The Best
Affirmations
Handbook

*Solutions to Actively Create
the Life Results You Want*

Dr. Patricia A. Ross
Scott Sharp Armstrong

New York

The Best Affirmations Handbook
Solutions to Actively Create the Life Results You Want

by Dr. Patricia A. Ross & Scott Sharp Armstrong

ISBN: 978-1-60037-555-2 Paperback

Library of Congress Control Number: 2008943795

Published by:

MORGAN · JAMES
THE ENTREPRENEURIAL PUBLISHER™

Morgan James Publishing, LLC
1225 Franklin Ave Ste 325
Garden City, NY 11530-1693
Toll Free 800-485-4943
www.MorganJamesPublishing.com

Cover & Interior Design by:
Heather Kirk
www.BrandedForSuccess.com

Habitat for Humanity®
Peninsula
Building Partner

A portion of the proceeds of the sale of this book will be donated to Habitat for Humanity.

Contact the authors at:
info@BestAffirmations.com

NOTE: Every attempt has been made by the authors to provide acknowledgement of the sources used for the material in this book. If there has been an omission please contact the authors.

Megan,
Always believe in yourself
and your dreams!

Dedication

For all the children

Acknowledgments

Patricia would like to thank her co-author, Scott Sharp Armstrong, for believing in her enough to ask her to work on this incredible project. I also want to thank my husband, W. D. Springsteel, who encouraged me from the beginning to push through and get this done—he knows the power of affirmations. Most especially, I want to thank my daughter, Zoë Willella—you are my daily inspiration. Your joy and ability to create keeps me uptone and moving ever upward. This book in large part is for you, cocomo.

Scott would like to thank the following people for their support and belief in this project: First of all I want to thank my co-author Dr. Ross for accepting my offer to co-author this exciting book. I appreciate you! Secondly, I want to thank my wife Sarah for all her support and unwavering encouragement throughout this project. I love you. Lastly I would like to thank the following people for believing in me: Dr. Paul Gluch, Robin Sharp, Robert Armstrong, Jeannie Kay Armstrong, and Dan Hawkins.

Together we would like to thank the Fab 5 radio gang, Tracy Repchuck, Frank Gasiorowski, and Dr. Mike Davidson for helping us launch Best Affirmations with style.

A special thank you goes to Terri Levine, the Guru of Coaching® who believes in our mission and continues to put Best Affirmations in front of all her loyal followers.

To Zebiba. Thank you for inspiring us to create the Affirmations for Africa foundation and for continually supporting Best Affirmations by handing our books out to all your amazing contacts!

To Dr. Robin Rushlo, "Networking with the Blind Guy," at www.BlogTalkRadio.com/blindguy, thank you for your enthusiasm and for giving us all that air time on your Gorilla Talk Radio program.

And last—because in many ways you are the most important: To Rhonda Del Baccio, "The Story Lady." Your generous spirit, your abundant heart—you are helping make our dreams a reality. Thank you!

Testimonials

"I have been studying affirmations for over twenty years, and nothing even comes close to the *Best Affirmations Handbook*! It is amazing!! As soon as I started using this handbook, it literally changed my life. Working with Scott's powerful affirmations helped to get me out of depression! They help to change my negative thinking and hold me accountable. This *Handbook* and its companion workbook have had an incredible impact on my life! Thanks, Patricia and Scott!!"

Karen Pietrowsky
Fitness Trainer, Rochester, Michigan

"The *Best Affirmations Workbook* is dynamite! Thirty days to change your life! It's worth its weight in gold!"

Dr. Paul Gluch
Professor, Author, Entrepreneur, San Clemente, California

"The *Best Affirmations Workbook* caught my attention immediately. I was so impressed by the content and its message, I ordered ten copies to pass out to my friends and family. This workbook is outstanding!"

Robin Sharp
Artist, Entrepreneur, Louisville, Colorado

"Best Affirmations has a thirty-day workbook which really made a difference for me. By actually following the daily instructions, I changed my thinking to a much more positive frame and learned to immediately switch negative intake into a positive track. Starting every day with a positive mindset brings positive things into fruition. I recommend this workbook for anyone who wants to accomplish more and feel good while doing so."

Sue Stinson
Author, R. N., Ottawa, Canada

"This *Handbook* is really helping me to keep my focus and believe in myself. The exercises are concise and only take a few minutes a day. I'd recommend it to anyone who really wants to fulfill their goals."

Mandy Carter
Singer, Song Writer, United Kingdom

"My thoughts at times are scattered: all over the place. The *Best Affirmations Workbook* helped me to get focus and be disciplined. It also helped me in overcoming negative self talk and negative words from other people. Through affirmations I learned to take action and it helped me overcome procrastination. This Affirmation workbook is priceless!"

Micheal Deaves
Entrepreneur, Ontario, California

"Using these affirmations has made a world of difference in my life in everything from having more self confidence to attracting more money and success. These affirmations are very powerful and, since starting to use them, I have been able to tap into my own Divine Intelligence for guidance in business decisions and creative inspiration. Thank you."

Brian Beshore
Author, Musician, Composer, Fontana, California

"Affirmations work! I practice them everyday and because they work, I'm dedicated to doing them often in a day! You can go through your day on autopilot, and have thoughts come and go, wondering: 'Why did I just think that, or why do I keep thinking that way about a particular situation or person or circumstance.' Affirmations help you change your intentional thinking. As soon as a negative thought creeps in, I zap it by saying my affirmations. I love how I feel when I say my affirmations. Plant good seeds of thought and you will reap the benefits of positive thinking everyday, all day."

Edward Raymond
Salesman, Ontairo, Canada

"The thirty-day workbook is fun and easy to use. I began to see results immediately! Right away I began to think differently. Quite simply, this workbook is awesome!"

Andy Odden
Teacher, Corvallis, Oregon

"Wow! This workbook is the GPS for the soul!!!"

Mark Oblinger
Business Owner, Musician, Composer, Boulder, Colorado

"My personal coach, Scott Armstrong, has made such a difference in how I look at things. What I've learned from him has totally transformed how I view success and personal transformation. He and his co-author Dr Patricia Ross, have written two books designed to help you get to the core of manifesting—a practical version of the Law of Attraction! The books are called the *Best Affirmations Handbook* and *The Best Affirmations Workbook*.

"The *Workbook* literally takes you by the hand and walks you step-by-step through a program that helps you master using affirmations to achieve your desires in life— any desires! As with all personal growth products I learn about, I'm always looking for proof before sharing my discovery with anyone.

"This workbook delivers everything it promises, big time! I can't believe how powerful and utterly simple the system is, but it works. Their ideas are based on over twenty years of research into the inner workings of the human mind and studying some of the most powerful techniques for personal change on the planet.

"Finally, and maybe for the first time ever, anyone who reads this book and does the daily exercises is just thirty days away from 'getting unstuck'—thirty days away from any goal! And they guarantee it!

"If you are at all interested in taking your life to the next level and are ready to become a master of your own life, then I urge you to not waste another moment. Check out this powerful program right now at BestAffirmations.com. You won't be disappointed!"

Liana Carbon
Author, Entrepreneur, San Diego, California

"This *Best Affirmation Handbook* has some powerful mojo! I've spent thousands of dollars on self-help materials, and this is one of the two best products I've ever purchased. My husband, who is always skeptical about what I do, read through a couple of the day's assignments and said, 'now this makes sense.' Even better—my twenty-year-old son, who won't read anything unless there's a video attached, saw the workbook on the computer, read through a couple of the day's assignments and immediately developed a list of ten top things he wanted to accomplish in his life! This is truly incredible. Thank you, Dr. Ross and Scott Armstrong. You are helping people become better and brighter human beings. Keep up the good work!"

Courtney Jones
Entrepreneur, Denver, Colorado

Table of Contents

Part One

Flipping the Decision Switch

Imagine that you are living the life that you have always wanted to. Go ahead—really get the whole picture of what that looks like. What kind of house do you live in? How do you spend your day? Where do you work, shop, and play? Where do you travel? Do you volunteer more because you can? Imagine everything, all of it. Really get the feeling—how does it feel to be living the life of your dreams? It feels great, doesn't it?

That's what the following folks did and this is what happened to them: Chet Ohrt, a Cardiovascular Technical Specialist, and his wife live in Vero Beach, Florida. He and his wife have also a house in Costa Rica. They put it out to the universe that they wanted to move there before the 2008 elections. (They actually found the house, their perfect beach house, using visualization.) Still they seemed glued to here because of their material ties and business.

At our suggestion, they taped, "We are moving to Costa Rica by the elections" along with this affirmation: "we are going to sell Island Style"—the hair studio they owned on pieces of paper and hung them in various places around the house. Selling the studio would allow them to make the move to Costa Rica. Something interesting happened. They got a solid bite on the business, but then the potential buyer dropped out of the picture for three months. This prompted Chet's wife to get really specific with her affirmations. She wrote: "Kathleen (the potential buyer) is going to buy Island Style." This went up all over the house too. Every time doubt appeared, they would say, "it's all working its way out. When it happens it will be a surprise and will make us laugh." And they believed what they were saying utterly and completely. Not long after the last affirmation went up, out of the blue a signed contract appeared from this woman to our broker! It was a complete surprise to Chet and his wife—and it sure made them laugh and smile a lot!" Not only are they moving to Costa Rica but it's exactly on target, shortly after the elections! How's that for the power of creative intention?!

Then there is Laura Lee Devine, mother of three young children—two of whom are twins! —and an entrepreneur who owns her own yoga and Pilates studio. She told us that the tools we gave her really helped plant the seed to begin living her life with intention, conviction, and persistence towards what she wanted her story to convey. Each day she said she would look forward to learning and practicing a new affirmations tool, and each day she felt like she was discovering more of the buried treasure within her. She particularly enjoys involving her spouse and children in some of the exercises like The Morning Pep Rally and the Power of Laughter. She noticed how she could instantly raise her vibrations as she ran around screeching her affirmations with enthusiasm and such excitement! Ten months after starting her affirmations program, Laura Lee could clearly see the connection between what Best Affirmations teaches to living in the moment and making the most of each moment she has to spend!

And if that isn't inspiring enough, here is perhaps our favorite story about the power of affirmations because it is so dramatic. Gerard Manley is a financial advisor who lives in Dublin, Ireland. The location alone could pull someone down into the dumps, but Gerard chose to travel a different path. He told us, "I've had tremendous success using affirmations! I use 'I attract sales from both known and unknown sources,' everyday. Without your handbook I would not use affirmations. I had stopped using affirmations and now that I am using them again, they are really helping. This is a very tough period in my work life. I lost my job, am owed money for software that I created; my wife's car has just died. This is all very stressful, yet despite all of these real hardships things are going my way. It is extraordinary."

Now, some of you will think after reading these affirmation success stories, "this totally excites me. It revs my engines, gets me jumping up and down with joy." However, many of you think, "this could never happen even though I want it to," and so you spend another day just slogging through, having some success, but mostly just getting by.

Why?! What has just happened? Why are some of you feeling totally pumped up and some of you are feeling more than a little deflated? The reason is both of you have just made an affirmation. In other words, you both told yourself what you can expect to experience because of what you think. Those of you who are jazzed made this affirmation: "creating the life I want totally excites me." However, some of you made the other affirmation, the one that says: "the life I really want can never happen." And guess what, whatever you think is exactly what is going to happen to you.

For some of you, you may be new to the idea of affirmations, and you are in a great position. You get to find out how they work from the very beginning! For many of you, there's a good chance that you've been through a lot of personal development programs. You may have heard or read that affirmations are supposed to work, but you've never found that they really help you. There are a couple of reasons for that.

First, many of you might have problems with affirmations simply because you don't really understand how they work. To understand a concept, it is vital to understand the words in it. Have you ever wondered why they are called "affirmations"? We asked the same question ourselves and this is what we found. The root or base word of "affirmation" is actually "affirm" and it means to say something positively. It also means to declare firmly and assert something to be true. So, at a very basic level, an affirmation is when you say something is true.

And this gives you the reason why affirmations work. Affirmations are powerful because they are thoughts. Thoughts are powerful because *thoughts create reality*. You have to have the idea of something before you make it happen in the physical universe. You have to have the idea, the thought that you can create your own company, for example, before you begin the process of making it happen.

The bottom line is you create things first—literally the events, the "luck," all the manifestations of reality—with your thoughts. So whatever you think is true! Think about this for a minute. It doesn't matter if the thought is positive or negative; whatever you think is what you create. Period.

This idea is *huge*! For some of you, the idea that what you think is what you create might actually be scary, but it isn't, really. It is the most empowering, amazing, life-creating and life-changing statement there is.

Now we've had people tell us that affirmations are just putting a positive "fluff" on bad things and so somehow, you're not fully confronting everything that is going on in your life. *Nothing* could be further from the truth. Affirmations actually help you to take full responsibility for your life for *all* that happens. If something bad is happening in your life, you take active responsibility for it because you know that your thoughts are in part or in whole creating it and—more empowering—you can actively do something positive about it. On the flip side, if good things are happening in your life, you take pride in knowing that *you* created it.

There are too many of you who want to better your life, and may even know some of the tools that can help you change your life, but you are stuck. We want to help you get out of that rut because we know, deep in our hearts, that if you are creating the life you want by choice, our world would be a better and saner one for everyone! So go ahead, create as many good, positive things as you can in your life and in those lives around you!

MAKE AFFIRMATIONS WORK FOR YOU

Many of you who are reading this know that you should do affirmations everyday, all the time. (For those of you who are new to this wonderful game of affirmations, that is rule number one: you do affirmations everyday, all the time!) But too many of you don't. The reason why this is true leads to the other reason why too many of you haven't been able to make affirmations work for you.

For you see, up until this point, no-one has ever presented you with a comprehensive set of tools to get you going! This is exactly what has been missing from many of the other personal development programs.

We did some research and found that while there are many good self-help books written that include affirmations, none of them take you through a step-by-step program to help you create a lasting habit of saying affirmations! So, since necessity is the mother of invention, we created a handbook that does exactly that for you!

And here it is: the *Best Affirmations Handbook*! To create it, we took the decades of our combined wisdom and experience with affirmations, looked at what worked and what didn't, and put it all together in an easy to follow guide. We've created a program that pulls together all of our knowledge about affirmations, all of our tools that we have, the ones that we know work. It is a step-by-step guide, something that comes with a contract that you sign with yourself, promising yourself that you are going to do this program and stay committed.

What it comes down to is that you need to commit to changing your life. Go ahead. Say this out loud: "Today, I commit to changing my life." And the process is so much fun! You will laugh, learn, and fall in love with you as a beautiful being who is able to take control of your destiny and create all that you desire.

NEVER TURN DOWN OPPORTUNITY

"Greatness begins by saying *yes*! to an opportunity." This is an affirmation. It is a thought that can guide your decisions.

Dr. Patricia Ross and Scott Sharp Armstrong might not be working together to bring you this handbook if Scott didn't already have that affirmation firmly planted in his head. He had asked Patricia to edit his book, *Boston Marathon or Bust: A Proven Step-by-Step Program to Help you Change Your Life, Sports, and Business Goals in Record Time* (www.BostonmarathonorBust.com). Five people had already looked at it. "It will only take you a couple of hours" he said, with confidence. Patricia looked over the first ten pages and found that the book wasn't ready for publication at all. She made a lot of suggested changes, so many that Scott almost said "thanks but no thanks." But then he remembered the affirmation about saying "yes" to opportunity, and he listened to what Patricia was saying about a good editor. He decided to work with her, and the rest, as the saying goes, is history.

And what a history! Scott has been using affirmations because he knows their power, and through affirmations he has achieved amazing things in his life. He qualified for and then ran the one hundredth running of the Boston Marathon. He has become one of the world's top success coaches, helping hundreds of people achieve their dreams. And it was because of saying his affirmations everyday and all the time that his book is now published by one of the fastest growing publishing companies in the world and is a popular title on Amazon, attracting world-wide attention. He also helped Patricia see the power of her gift, and because of his book, she became first an editor then as a writing and success coach earning hundreds of dollars an hour.

Now we want to share these tools with you because we also share another deep passion: we want to make this world a happier, better place. We're doing this in part with this book by helping people change their mindset, to find the riches of life that each one of us can acquire by thinking strong, positive thoughts. But we also want to help those who are less fortunate than we are. From the moment we conceived of Best Affirmations, we knew that we wanted to give back, and so we created Affirmations for Africa, which is dedicated to getting this book into the hands of everyone in Africa who wants it. But we're not stopping there. We want to bring it home again with Affirmations for America, an organization dedicated to getting the word out about affirmations to children everywhere in America.

Most important, however, is we want to help you because we know that when one person changes his or her mindset, then that person can go and help somebody else. When you help yourself, you are then in a position to help others change their lives, and the "pay it forward" concept just keeps it growing and growing. Our philosophy is we succeed when you succeed. Who said world peace isn't possible?

YOUR CHALLENGE

Affirmations are powerful. In this handbook, you are going to hear stories about many different, highly successful people, who have used affirmations to help them take their lives to whole new levels of success.

Just to give you a taste—one of our favorites is about Tracy Repchuk. You will be learning more about Tracy's ideas of using affirmations to take you through a quantum leap, a leap in your business and/or your life that is so fast and so successful that it will amaze you! Here is Tracy's story: in January 2007, she started her Internet marketing company. Within five months, she had made over $96,353, wrote and became a bestselling author, got her book picked up internationally, and won "New Internet Marketing Success of the Year" from the World Internet Mega Summit with an all-expense paid trip to Singapore and a speaking engagement in front of thirty-four hundred people. All this started with affirmations, and Tracy continues to say affirmations everyday all the time so that she's always in the mindset to create her dreams.

Many of us know that we need to do affirmations, but why is it that we don't do them everyday like all the books and self-help guys tell us to?

This handbook answers that question.

To make this the *best* handbook for you, we have pooled all of our resources taken from years of research, study and, most important, actual application. We have included the best of the best—the best affirmations, the best techniques. You will hear about people who have used this program and how different steps worked well for them.

If you take the time to really learn how to execute the tools we give you here; if you pay attention to the tips we offer you throughout, then you will see immediate results. Your life and your thoughts will be changed forever. We guarantee that! The tools that we give you have worked for us and for our clients around the world, and we know they will work for you! The time to act is now. Buddha taught that "all that we are is the result of what we have thought."

Remember, greatness begins by saying *yes*! to an opportunity. You need to ask yourself this question: if you don't start doing something different now, what's it all going to be like in a month, six months, or a year from now? How will you feel, doing the same old thing? Will you be happy?

There's a powerful definition of insanity: doing the same thing over and over, but when things don't work out, you still do the same thing but you expect different results. Don't get caught in this trap.

For things to change, you have to change. For things to get better, you have to get better. Are you ready to have a better life—the life of your dreams?

Part Two
The Makeup of Affirmations

Knowledge is power.
—Michele Foucault

Well done! You have taken the first step to discovering the real power of affirmations. Before you actually start learning the various tools in this handbook, however, it is vital that you study this section carefully. (It is actually the action step that you do on day one, and because Patricia is a teacher at heart, there is a quiz at the end. So pay attention. Your future depends on it!)

Part two is simply an explanation of why and how affirmations work. Research has found that when you understand the why and the how of affirmations, they work better.

The explanation is that simple. When you really understand something, you know it and can use it. We want you to be able to use the tools that we give you in the hand-book, and so we really want you to understand how they work. And, yes, we have that ulterior motive. We want you to be successful in this program because we want you to go and help others be successful as well. You are better prepared to be a teacher yourself if you know more about the ins and outs of affirmations.

Jack Canfield, co-author of *Chicken Soup for the Soul,* tells a story he read about the highly successful actor/comedian Jim Carrey. When Jim Carrey first came to Hollywood, he didn't have a dime to his name. But, he knew he was talented, and he also knew about the power of affirmations. The first thing he did was write a check to himself for $1 million and then put the intention there that one day in the near future he would be able to cash it. Then, everyday he would drive up Mulholland Drive, look out at the city of Los Angeles, stretch out his arms and say: "Everybody wants to work with me. I'm a really good actor. I have all kinds of great movie offers " He would repeat these things over and over literally convincing himself that he had a couple of movies lined up. As he would drive down that hill, he felt ready to take the world on. And as he drove, he would say over and over: "Movie offers are out there for me, I just don't hear them yet." (Canfield took this story from *Movieline,* July 1994.)

We all know how famous Jim Carrey is. This story tells us that he got where he is because he had the right mind-set, and he created that mindset with affirmations.

WHAT IS AN AFFIRMATION?

Affirmations, really, are simple. They are short, power-ful statements. When you say them or think them or even hear them, they become the thoughts that create your real-ity. Affirmations, then, are your conscious thoughts. But it really goes one step further—and this is important, so pay attention: affirmations are you being in *conscious* control of your thoughts.

Research has shown that we have between forty-five thousand and fifty-one thousand thoughts a day. That's about one hundred and fifty to three hundred thoughts a minute. Research has also shown that for most people 80 percent of those thoughts are negative.

Now, we have been taught to think that most of these fifty-one thousand thoughts are "sub-conscious" thoughts meaning that they are below our conscious awareness level. We want to present to you this fact: ***Affirmations actually make your sub-conscious thoughts conscious***. Affirmations make you consciously aware of your thoughts. When you start making conscious positive thoughts, you actually become more aware of the negative thoughts that are always threatening to take over.

It's an interesting phenomenon, really. It actually proves true what your mother always warned: be careful of what you wish for because that is what you get. She was basically telling you that you create what you think about.

When you're not aware of your thoughts, they tend to be negative. *Not* being aware of your thoughts tends to cause a nasty spiral downward. Remember that 80 percent figure of negative thoughts? It gets worse. Whatever you are thinking about, 90 percent gets carried over to the next day's fifty-one thousand thoughts. So if you're thinking negative thoughts, you will cause yourself to think more negative thoughts. This is not going to get you out of your rut.

Affirmations can change all of that! Affirmations make you conscious of your thoughts. In part one, we gave you the definition of *affirm*. Here is it again, because it is key to all that we're talking about:

To *affirm* means to say something positively. It means to declare firmly and assert something to be true.[1]

Affirmations are statements where you assert that what you want to be true *is* true.

HOW AFFIRMATIONS WORK

The simple explanation for how affirmations work is that our universe works in a very specific way. Before you can make something happen in the physical universe, you first have to have the thought or consideration that you want that thing to happen. Think about it. Before you make a phone call or pet your dog or kiss your baby you have to **decide** that you're going to do that. Affirmations are the decisions that you make to have something happen. They must be there in order for you to then begin the process of making whatever you want to happen in the physical universe actually happen.

To put it another way: Affirmations are simply you being in control of your thoughts, declaring to the universe what you want to be true. And when you want it to be true, it will be true because that is your intention.

THE POWER OF INTENTION

Intention is the power behind affirmations. When you assert something to be true, it is true because your intention makes it true.

Webster's dictionary defines intention as the "conception of a thing formed first by the direct application of the mind to the individual object, idea or image."[2] This is what we were just talking about. You need to have the conception of a thing in your mind; you must have the intention to make something happen before it actually happens.

There's also something really quirky about intention. It is very important to be very clear about what it is you want. It's like Chet Ohrt and his wife. Their affirmations really started working when they got really specific— when they named the person they wanted to buy their hair salon.

It's simple. The clearer you are, the more your intention will come into reality. If you want five new clients, put that intent out to the universe. If you want those five new clients to be $1,000 clients as opposed to $200 clients, then make sure that is what you intend. Remember, clarity is power.

AFFIRMATIONS AND THE LAW OF ATTRACTION

Because of *The Secret*, the DVD and book that tells the story of a woman who wanted to find out why some people were successful and others not, many people are very aware of something called the Law of Attraction. If you haven't seen or read *The Secret*, we highly recommend that you do so, but the following will help you understand what the Law of Attraction is and why it is so closely connected to affirmations.

The Law of Attraction is a natural law of the universe and it is actually a very simple concept. At its most basic, it is "like attracts like." Whatever you are thinking about, that is what you attract in your life. Bob Doyle in *The Secret* defines it this way: the law of attraction is impersonal. It does not see "good" or "bad." It is a law of the universe that simply receives your thoughts and then reflects those thoughts back to you as your life experience.[3]

---

1 *Webster's Ninth New Collegiate Dictionary*, s.v. "affirm."

2 *Webster's Ninth New Collegiate Dictionary*, s.v. "intention."

3 Byrne, Rhonda. *The Secret*. New York: Atria Books, 2006.

The law of attraction simply gives you whatever it is you are thinking about.

Also in *The Secret*, John Assaraf talks about a problem that many people have. Most people, he says, think about what they don't want, and then they wonder why that thing they don't want shows up over and over again.

The answer to this is startlingly simple. Assaraf says: "The only reason why people do not have what they want is because they are thinking more about what they *don't* want than what they *do* want."

Assaraf's advice is simple. "Listen to your thoughts, and listen to the words you are saying."[4] Because the Law of Attraction is absolute, there are no mistakes. In other words, this law works every time, no matter what. Whatever you are thinking about is what you are going to attract.

So, the question is: why attract what you *don't* want when it is just as easy to think about what you *do* want? The choice is yours.

THE POWER OF CHOICE

Even though we don't always want to admit it, we have a choice about how we feel and how we act. When something less than positive happens in our lives, we can either choose to get all balled up about it and do nothing or we can face up to it and work to change it for the better. The same holds true for emotions. We really are masters of our emotions. Try this sometime. When you're really angry with your partner, just stop and smile and see what happens. (One of the Best Affirmations tools deals with exactly this issue, so you'll get some practice at it.)

---

4 Byrne, Rhonda. *The Secret*. New York: Atria Books, 2006.

Affirmations give us the ability to believe that we can choose to change those things we need to. Need to lose weight? You can either choose to moan and groan about it but do nothing or do those things necessary to make weight loss happen—getting the right mindset and then exercising more and eating less.

You can choose to be happy, sad, upset, exhilarated—name your emotion—about anything. You can also choose to act or not act. With affirmations, because you become conscious of your thoughts, you're more able and thus willing to choose to have positive thoughts about whatever situation you find yourself in. When you have a positive mindset, you're more willing and able to take action. And *that* is a winning combination: positive thought with action!

THE LAW OF VIBRATION

When you choose to think positively, then you also positively activate the companion law to the law of attraction. It is the Law of Vibration.

To vibrate means to move backwards and forwards, to shake, swing, or waver, to quiver or to cause to quiver. How this works with affirmations is best explained by a simple device called a tuning fork. This is what musicians use to get the right note to tune their instruments. Guitar players and violinists use them all the time.

They work this way: You hit this fork against something, and it gives you a musical note. This note is caused by the vibration of the metal moving back and forth very quickly. But this is the interesting part. If you hold a tuning fork that is not vibrating next to something that is playing the same note, the fork will start to vibrate. It is acting according to the Law of Vibration which is any entity, living or non-living, will respond to something best if that something has the same vibration.

This becomes important when you consider the fact that one of the very highest forms of energy is thought. Every thought that you think has a vibration. Anger, fear, being a victim, these are all negative thoughts and they have a low vibration. Interest, enthusiasm, and even the will to create, all have high vibrations. Now this is important: every thought that you think has a vibration that goes out to the universe and finds a vibration to match.

If the vibration is low, the universe is going to match with something low: problems, worry, and all that nasty stuff. When the vibration is high, the universe will comply and match it with something high: abundance, prosperity, happiness.

When you say affirmations, you are creating a specific vibration. This is what we talk about when we say an affirmation needs to "resonate" with you. To *resonate* means that two things have the same vibration, so when we say, "find an affirmation that resonates with you," we mean, find an affirmation that hits your same vibration point. The more you believe in your affirmation, the more it resonates. The more the affirmation resonates with you, the higher the vibration between you and the affirmation gets. The higher the vibration, the more you will find good positive things coming into your life.

This is why affirmations are so powerful!

POSITIVE SELF-EXPECTANCY

Jack Canfield, co-author of *Chicken Soup for the Soul*, talks a lot about positive self-expectancy in his book, *The Success Principles*. Basically, positive self-expectancy is a fancy way of saying *you get what you expect.* If you just thought, that's just like the law of attraction, it is. They are two sides of the same coin, but positive self-expectancy is a great way to show you how the law of attraction and intention work together.

For you see, expectation is actually very closely related to intention. When you expect something to happen, you are really just putting out the intention that it will.

In his book, Canfield tells a true story that totally clarifies the idea of how this all works together.[5]

There was a group of doctors in Texas who were studying the effect of arthroscopic knee surgery and the power of expectation. It's a classic story of the placebo effect. The doctors assigned patients with sore, worn-out knees to one of three surgical procedures: scraping out the knee joint, washing out the joint, or doing nothing.

During the "nothing" operation, doctors anesthetized the patient, made three incisions in the knee as if to insert their surgical instruments, and then pretended to operate. Two years after surgery, the doctors found something startling. Patients who underwent the pretend surgery reported the same amount of relief from pain and swelling as those who had received the actual treatments. The person expected the "surgery" to improve the knee, and it did.

So positive self-expectancy is you expecting good things to happen and so you then have the intention of having good things happen. The key, of course, is to keep your expectations and your intentions positive.

5 Canfield, Jack. *The Success Principles: How to Get from Where You Are to Where You Want to Be.* New York: HarperCollins, 2005. Story originally appeared in *The New England Journal of Medicine.* 2002. 347(2). 81-88, 132-133.

AFFIRMATIONS TAKE YOU THROUGH THE QUANTUM LEAP

The final idea that we want to present to you before you get started on your affirmation journey is one that is taken from physics. In part one, we gave you Tracy Repchuk's story. She took a quantum leap in her life, and this is what that means.

The quantum universe is the one that scientists can't quite measure. They see the effects of what they termed "quantum physics," everywhere in our universe, but they can't measure it like they can measure light waves or the speed of sound.

A quantum leap in terms of physics, then, is the explosive jump that a particle of matter undergoes in moving from one place to another. Particles make these jumps without apparent effort (that's one of the reasons why physicists can't measure them), and, even more amazingly, they make these jumps without covering all the bases. When we do something, there are steps that we take to get us from the start through to the finish. A quantum leap means that you went from the start to the finish and skipped a lot if not all of the steps in between.

How does this work with affirmations? Tracy, along with Fred Allen Wolf, author of the award winning *Taking a Quantum Leap* have picked up this idea and have applied it to affirmations. They both recognize this: if you do affirmations in the right way, saying them everyday with intention and positive feelings, they will take you through the quantum leap!

You can get what your heart desires and it doesn't have to take forever! Quantum leaps are fun! They can fit years into months, and you create quantum leaps—whether they are you making a million dollars, slimming down to your ideal weight, or just being a better parent—by doing your affirmations daily and doing them correctly.

****

What we hope for you is that your life changes in a great way for the better. We want you to have a more successful, positive, abundant and happy life. Even if you just take a couple of the tools that we offer you, then we feel that we have given you some success and therefore we are successful.

So take a moment to prepare yourself because you are about to embark on one of the best, most creative, and definitely one of the most enjoyable adventures of your life!

You are an incredibly powerful being who can create anything you want. It is *you* who puts the intention into affirmations. *You* are the one that puts the charge, the volts, the power into your affirmation. You are the one who takes you through the quantum leap to ultimate success!!

Our job is to help you tap into that power by helping make you conscious of your thoughts and then turning those thoughts into something positive.

Are you ready?
Turn the page and may you finally start to live
the life you have always wanted.

Part Three

Change Your Life: The Best Affirmations Solutions

Jim Rohn, the man who has mentored many well known success coaches said, "With every disciplined effort, there is a multiple reward." Discipline is the key word here. This handbook offers you the "best of the best," the best tools that we've found work in making affirmations happen, and the best advice that we have given our clients over the years.

But the quality of the material is only as good as the effort you put into it. And your effort is driven by your commitment and your discipline. Affirmations work, but it's up to you to make them work.

This handbook contains thirty affirmation tools. Each tool has two parts: an Affirmation Action Step and an End-of-the-Day Power Affirmation. Read through the

Affirmation Action Step for the day and then at the end of the day, say your End-of-the-Day Power Affirmation out loud. Shake the rafters with it. It will not only end your day on a wonderful high note, but also reaffirm that your affirmations are doing their job.

STEP ONE

Commit to working through each tool at least once. Try everything. Find out what works for you. Some tools you will like more than others, and that is okay. The most important point is that you need to discover what tools help you get into the *habit of positive thinking.* That is our goal for you, and that is why you will find that ultimately, everything that we ask you to do is simply a different way to get you into the habit of saying affirmations all the time, every day.

Remember Jim Carrey? He did his affirmations all the time, and look where he is now! And there are millions of others who have known about and used the power of affirmations. Tap into that power!

STEP TWO

Follow the directions, and no matter what we ask you to do, keep saying your affirmations. Each day builds on and adds to the preceding days. Know that you are building a solid foundation for success. Also, there are a few times when we have you write your affirmations. We do this for a reason. There is a huge power in writing something down. It actually makes that thought more tangible, more real to you and to the universe. It strengthens the idea that this is what you want.

STEP THREE

Keep going, even when things get tough. Sometimes you might find yourself not wanting to follow through. Some of you might even want to just throw your hands up and quit. We've all been there. A little persistence and discipline at this point can change your life forever.

So if you find that you do not want to try everything that is offered in this handbook, this is what you need to do:

Action Step A:

Make sure that you understand everything that you have read. If you find there is something that you don't understand, it is because there is a word or words that you don't know. Find the word that is confusing to you and look it up in a good dictionary.

Action Step B:

You need to acknowledge that negativity might be getting you down. You might still be focusing too much on negative things, like how many bills you have piled up, or the huge dental bill that you are going to have to face because your tooth hurts and it's not going to be ignored.

As you do this program, know that handling the negativity that comes up is vital. Sometimes all a person needs to do is simply acknowledge that the negativity is there and then decide to just keep thinking positively. The positive thinking will help you figure out how to handle the negative situation. It really is a little like magic!

You are changing your life, and sometimes change can be uncomfortable. Working to maintain a positive attitude and create new and wondrous things in your life with that positive attitude can cause you to get overwhelmed sometimes. Negativity can hit at all the wrong times, and it seems to like to come up when things are going well. There are forces in the universe that do not want you to succeed. Part of forming the habit of positive thinking through affirmations is handling the negativity without letting it get you down. We give you three different ways to handle negativity in the workbook, but we wanted to address it here because negative thoughts, either from yourself or from others, can cause you to fail. We want you to succeed!

Remember you have an average of fifty thousand thoughts a day. You want to make them conscious. Millions of people around the world have changed their lives, literally, with affirmations. When you are committed, there's always a way.

STEP FOUR

Remember, the universe rewards action. As you are saying your affirmations, make sure that you are also adding action to back up what you are thinking. If you are affirming that "I have three new clients today," then you need to make the phone calls or write the e-mails that will get you those three new clients.

STEP FIVE

Once you have really learned how to use affirmations so that they really do work for you, feel free to pass it on. Share this wealth of information with your family and friends.

Our motto: *The more people who are living conscious lives, and the more self- fulfilled and happier people are, the better off everyone is!*

Really understanding the power of affirmations makes you more conscious. You are thinking consciously and creatively when you make affirmations a part of your everyday, habitual thinking. We really are committed to making this world a better place. So "pay it forward." Get your family and friends affirming positive thoughts daily. They will thank you, and so will we!

Are you ready to start?

Good!

Start! And may your life never be the same again!

P.S.: If you find that you need extra help getting through the program, please visit www.bestaffirmations.com. There you will find the companion workbook: *Best Affirmations Workbook: The 30-day How to Guide to Actively Create the Life You Want.* It is an actual thirty-day program that takes you through all the tools we offer here, but it acts like a coach, holding you accountable, and ensuring that you get through the program!

P.P.S.: If you know you really want to complete the program, but you can't do it on your own, please let us know! Go to www.bestaffirmationscoach.com and find out how to get a twenty-minute free consultation with Scott, Patricia, or one of their top-notch coaches.

Getting Started

*What we are today comes from our
thoughts of yesterday, and our present
thoughts build our life of tomorrow:
Our life is the creation of our mind.*

—Buddha

As we promised you in part two, your first task in this workbook is to study, really study, how affirmations work. The reason for this is simple: we have found through years of experience that when you really understand the why and the how of affirmations, then you will have more success with them.

To study means to look at something closely, to ask questions, and to not only read but also really understand what you're reading.

You will then be asked to set goals and sign a contract. We know that if you don't set goals, you aren't as likely to finish, and the contract is a way for you to firmly decide that you are going to make it through this program.

Oh, and make sure to have fun with all of this!

Affirmation Action Step #1:

➤ Say this affirmation:

I know that when I start changing my thoughts, I can change my destiny, my life, forever.

➤ Study part two of this book.

Make sure that you understand all the words and concepts.

➤ Take the following short quiz.

Reference part one and part two as much as you need. The purpose of this exercise is for you to feel good about what you know.

1. What is the definition of ***affirmation***?

   a. To do whatever you want.

   b. To think that everyone has it better than you do.

   c. To say something positively, assert something to be true.

2. Who holds the power of making affirmations come true?

   a. You.

   b. The mailman.

   c. Your mother.

3. What is the Law of Attraction?

    a. You're really attracted to your partner.

    b. If you think positive thoughts, you will attract positive things.

    c. If you think positive thoughts, you will attract negative things.

4. True or False: Affirmations involve you being in conscious control of your thoughts.

5. What is the relationship between the law of vibration and the concept of resonance?

    a. The earth is moving at a different speed than Mars.

    b. You have an energy that moves at a certain rate and the things that you like best are the things that match that energy.

    c. Energy and reasoning have no relationship to each other.

6. If you think negative thoughts, what are you going to get?

7. True or False: You must have the intention to do something or believe something before anything can happen in the physical universe.

(Answers for the quiz are on the following page.)

➤ Set a Goal for this Program:

   On a scale of one to five, five being the highest, rate where you are right now—

_____ Emotionally

_____ Physically

_____ Mentally

_____ Spiritually

➤ Using the above scale as a guide, write down where you would ultimately like to be emotionally, physically, mentally, and spiritually.

➤ Now, write down three to five of your biggest successes or highlights in your life. These are your success reference points. They help set you up to really believe that you can achieve anything that you want to.

➤ Finally, write down at least three things that you want to accomplish in the next thirty days as you read through this handbook. This is your goal.

Answers to quiz: 1c, 2a, 3b, 4T, 5b, 6 negative thoughts, 7T.

YOUR CONTRACT

One last thing: Say the following out loud and then sign the contract in the space provided. Your signature indicates that you are committed to finishing this program.

I will not settle for any thing other than achieving the life of my dreams. I promise myself that I will do all the tools in this handbook to the best of my abilities. No matter what happens, how many roadblocks get in my way, I am committed to actively working on this program, no ifs, ands, or buts.

Your Name _____ Date_____

Making an Affirmations Box

*Nurture your mind with great
thoughts, for you will never go any
higher than you think.*

—Benjamin Disraeli

Organization is always important to any endeavor.
When you keep your desk or table free from clutter,
it helps keep your mind free from clutter as well. This next
step is to get you organized, so you have a place to keep
all of your favorite affirmations.

Patricia found this step to be especially helpful because
her desk sometimes gets messy. (She has so much happening, and she has a two-year-old!) She had all these great
affirmations lying about because she would write them
down when she heard them. But when she really needed
one, she would have to go searching for it.

Affirmations are just like your favorite recipes. You get them from all sorts of different places, and it is nice to have them organized in one place so that you don't have to go searching for them when you need them.

Affirmation Action Step #2:

➤ Today you are going to make an Affirmations Box. It's just like a recipe box; it uses all the same stuff. You will need to get:

✦ a 3" × 5" recipe card box

✦ 3" × 5" note cards

✦ card dividers

➤ On the card dividers, write down each category of your life that you want to change—finances, spiritual, health, time management etc. (If you need some help coming up with areas, visit www.bestaffirmations.com and see the list of categories on the left.)

➤ Next, write down the following affirmations, one on each card:

✦ I am confident!

✦ I am a brilliant business person.

✦ I deserve happiness, abundance, and prosperity.

✦ I have all the resources necessary to fulfill any and all of my life's goals.

✦ I am able to create anything that I want, now.

✦ Making money excites me and energizes me.

✦ My life is filled with joy, success, and abundance now!

- ✦ I am focused and persistent.

- ✦ My mind is always clear, focused, and energized.

- ✦ I can do anything I choose and get it done now.

- ✦ My affirmations attract amazing things in my life.

- ✦ My affirmations work, now!

➤ Now, file the affirmations under their appropriate heading.

➤ Once you made the box, pick one affirmation that really resonates with you. If none of these affirmations really work for you, please feel free to browse the web. There are tons of affirmations out there. We also provide twenty-two separate lists of affirmations at www.bestaffirmations.com. The most important part of this exercise is to find an affirmation that really works for you. Make sure that as you search for affirmations, you write them down on your cards and file them.

➤ Write your favorite affirmation on a 3x5 card.

➤ Carry this card with you all day, and every time you think about it, take the card out and read the affirmation out loud. Say it with feeling, with conviction. Say it like you know it is true. (You may not feel that it's true yet. Don't let that worry you. Just keep saying it with as much belief and conviction as you can muster!)

For the rest of the program, you are going to be using this box. Some days you will be adding to the box; some days you will be using affirmations that you have already written down. By the end of the program, we hope that you have a great central file of affirmations. You can even share it or make it a family heirloom!

And if you have children, get them involved. Let them help you put together your box. Let them draw on the outside, or draw pictures on the cards themselves. Affirmations are the epitome of creation; let your kids create with you!

END-OF-THE-DAY POWER AFFIRMATION:

Say this with *enthusiasm*: Congratulations (say your name or say self, whichever you're most comfortable with). I just had a terrific day with my affirmations program! My affirmations work. I feel awesome, able to create anything I desire. I am *unstoppable.*

How to Use Affirmations

SAY IT OVER AND OVER AND OVER AND OVER AND OVER AGAIN

*Thought is the sculptor who can create
the person you want to be.*
—Henry David Thoreau

The simplicity of affirmations is that the more you say them, the more you believe in them. The more you believe in them, the quicker they are going to happen. Remember, what you think is what you get! Today's task is to start the habit of saying your affirmations everyday, all the time.

Here's what can happen when you do this. Patricia was working with a realtor who was having problems with her business. She kept attracting people who were unethical and it was getting her down. Patricia told her to say, "I attract amazing, ethical people in my life," over and over. This realtor called Patricia three days later and said that the person who was really being a problem was no longer in her life, and she had three new leads with amazing people, people who were like her, willing and able to work and live ethical lives.

Affirmation Action Step #3:

➤ Pick the most important thing that you want to change in your life. Is it being more financially secure? Is it having more time or being more at peace with yourself?

➤ Find an affirmation that resonates with you best about this area. If it's one in your Affirmations Box, great. If none of those really resonate with you, find one that does and make sure to write it on its own 3x5 card.

➤ Say this affirmation at least one hundred times throughout the day. Have it become part of who you are fundamentally. If you can't keep track, say your affirmation ten times every hour for ten consecutive hours.

END-OF-THE-DAY POWER AFFIRMATION:

Say this with *intention*: Congratulations (say your name or say self, whichever you're most comfortable with). I just had a wonderful day with my affirmations program! My affirmations work. I feel awesome, able to create anything I desire. I am *unstoppable*.

The Power of Smiling

Always remember to be happy because you never know who's falling in love with your smile.
—Author Unknown

Smiling raises your vibration level. Period. It goes along with the fact that it takes far more muscles to frown than to smile. Frowning not only takes more effort, it pulls you down emotionally and spiritually. Do this quick exercise. Frown and feel the energy that goes with it. Now, smile, and feel the energy that goes with it. Big difference, huh?! Jacquelyn Aldana, author of the *15 Minute Miracle* reminds us to become the happiest person that we know. You will attract far more success in your life if you do.

Patricia had an amazing thing happen to her one morning. The first thing that she does when she wakes up is smile. She then says an affirmation. One morning, she woke up smiling and thought, "I'm going to make a million dollars today." Within two hours, she had a phone call where she learned that she was going to edit one of the best selling marketing series on the planet and making a substantial royalty for her effort. She knew instantly where that million dollars would be coming from.

Affirmation Action Step #4:

➤ Pick an affirmation that really resonates with you. If it's not from your Affirmations Box, make sure that you write it down on a card and then file it once you're done with this exercise.

➤ Tape the card to your bathroom mirror.

➤ Now comes the fun part. Smile at yourself for 60 seconds—really smile.

➤ Once you feel really happy, say your affirmation looking in the mirror with the most enthusiasm you ever had in your entire life. Say it at least 10 times in front of the mirror.

➤ Pick out two more affirmations and say those 10 times, in the same way, in front of the mirror.

Tip on handling negative thoughts: If you find yourself getting off track, if things are not working quite right, or if you're not where you want to be, force yourself to smile and say at least one affirmation three times.

END-OF-THE-DAY POWER AFFIRMATION:

Say this with *focus*: Congratulations (say your name or say self, whichever you're most comfortable with). I have just had a prosperous day with my affirmations program! My affirmations work. I feel awesome, able to create anything I desire. I am *unstoppable*.

Affirming that Affirmations Work

When you believe a thing,
believe in it all the way.

—Walt Disney

Intention is the power that lies behind affirmations. Intention is having your mind, your attention, and your will concentrated on some end or some purpose. Affirmations won't work if you don't put your intention behind them. This is actually a key step to this program.

Early on, Scott discovered how important this step really was. Once he started affirming that his affirmations work, then they started working all the time. Before he took this step, he found that there was a cycle that was going on that was not helping him create the life that he wanted. Before he started affirming that his affirmations work, he found that they would work sometimes, but then when the negativity came in, his affirmations wouldn't work.

Scott is constantly spotting this problem with his clients. They don't have the intention that their affirmations really work. The quick and powerful way to handle this is with the following:

Affirmation Action Step #5:

➤ Find your favorite place in or around your house, the place that makes you the happiest. Throw your arms wide open and say this with all the intention and passion you can:

My affirmations work!

➤ Say it again at least ten times, each time with intention, passion, and enthusiasm: all those things that raise your vibration level.

➤ On a note card, write the following:

✦ My affirmations work!

✦ I believe that my affirmations work no matter what!

✦ I have absolute certainty and confidence that my affirmations work for me.

➤ Say each of these affirmations over and over until you find that you really believe them. This might take ten or more times, but that's okay. The important point is to really get the feeling that your affirmations work!

Tip on Handling the Negative: There might be a little voice inside you that's saying: "this isn't true." Know two things about this voice. One: it's yours. Take ownership for it; acknowledge that it is you thinking that thought. Then, know that because it is you, you can easily change your voice to a positive one. It's you who changes the negative to the positive. It's you who decides to either let the habitual negative thoughts come into play or to shut the negativity down and think positively. Put your attention on the positive, and positive thoughts will quickly override the negative ones!

END-OF-THE-DAY POWER AFFIRMATION:

Say this with *a feeling of persistence*: Congratulations (say your name or say self, whichever you're most comfortable with). I have just finished an outstanding day with my affirmations program! My affirmations work. I feel awesome, able to create anything I desire. I am *unstoppable*.

Handling Negative Thoughts

*The greatest discovery of my generation
is that a human being can alter his life
by altering his attitudes.*

—William James

While we have been giving you some hints on handling the negative feelings and vibrations as they come up, today you're going to learn our favorite tool for handling negativity.

Scott has his coaching clients with negative thought patterns do this as one of their first assignments. Within the first couple of days the negative thinking disappears! Scott is always a little amazed at how incredibly well this technique works!

Affirmation Action Step #6:

➤ Get two or three of your favorite affirmations ready. Remember, if they don't come from your Affirmations Box, make sure to write them on cards and then file them at the end of the day.

➤ Find a rubber band that you can wear comfortably around your wrist. Put it on.

➤ When you find yourself having a negative thought at any point in the day, snap the rubber band, and then say an affirmation.

➤ A variation on this is to snap the rubber band and then think about a great success you've had, or something really fun you did. Whichever version you choose (and by all means, do them both if both work!), you are reminding yourself every time you snap the rubber band that you need to constantly think positive thoughts.

END-OF-THE-DAY POWER AFFIRMATION:

Say this with *conviction*: Congratulations (say your name or say self, whichever you're most comfortable with). I just had an excellent day with my affirmations program! My affirmations work. I feel awesome, able to create anything I desire. I am *unstoppable*.

The Law of Attraction

*You must begin to think of yourself as
becoming the person you want to be.*
—David Viscott

Affirmations work hand in hand with the Law of Attraction. Remember the lessons from *The Secret*? The only reason why people don't have what they want is that they are constantly thinking about what they *don't* want. The Law of Attraction works either negatively or positively. It is only activated by what you are thinking. Affirmations are getting you to think about what you *do* want. When you say them every day, all the time, you are making the Law of Attraction work for you in positive ways.

The Law of Attraction is at work in everyone's lives, even children. One of Patricia's clients was preparing for her college entrance exam, the ACT. This student kept saying: "I don't test well." "I can't take standardized tests." "I'm not smart enough for this." That activated the negative side of the Law of Attraction and, sure enough, she kept scoring far lower than her ability. One assignment that Patricia gave her was to say the following affirmations at least three times every day: "I test well." "I'm intelligent and can think through any question on the ACT," and "I take standard-ized tests with ease and confidence." It wasn't long before her scores started moving up, and her final scores were far better than she or her parents ever expected!

It is really important to get that today's assignment is to really focus on the things you want. Keep your mind off the things you don't want.

Affirmation Action Step #7:

➤ Write down the five things that you really want right now. Get the feeling that you accomplished that goal.

➤ Write down affirmations that say that these five things are accomplished. For example, "I now have a full schedule of clients" or "I am able to create whatever income I desire."

➤ Write down your new affirmations on note cards.

➤ Say each affirmation at least five times each, and file them in your box.

END-OF-THE-DAY POWER AFFIRMATION:

Say this with *enthusiasm*: Congratulations (say your name or say self, whichever you're most comfortable with). I just had an amazing day with my affirmations program! My affirmations work. I feel awesome, able to create anything I desire. I am *unstoppable*.

Finding the Right Vibration

*A man can succeed at almost anything
for which he has unlimited enthusiasm.*
—Charles Schwab

Up to this point, we have been prompting you to say your affirmations with strong, positive feelings and a belief that they will work. The reason for this is simple. If you say one affirmation with total feeling, it is the equivalent of saying the same affirmation 100 times without feeling. To get your affirmations to really work, you need to get the right feeling, the right vibration. When you really get the feeling behind the affirmation you're saying, when your vibration is high, you have hooked into the positive aspect of the Law of Attraction.

Patricia also uses this exercise with her young clients. One problem students have is that they are bored with the exercises given them. This is especially true for many of their language arts and history assignments as well as the reading sections on most standardized tests. In order to combat this, she has her students do a version of the following exercise to show them that when their vibration is running high about a certain reading passage or a certain exercise, they are able to keep their focus better and thus do better on the assignments.

Affirmation Action Step #8:

➤ Find some way to record yourself. This can be with an inexpensive tape recorder or with your MP3 player.

➤ Pick one of your favorite affirmations.

➤ Say this affirmation with absolutely no feeling. Be bored; don't really care about it. Note how that makes you feel.

➤ Next, say the same affirmation with the feeling that it's never going to actually work, that what you are saying isn't true. Note how that makes you feel.

➤ Next, say the affirmation with a little bit of interest. Not much, just a little. Be conservative about how you say it. Note how you feel.

➤ Now, say the affirmation with a lot of interest. Note how you feel

➤ Finally, say the affirmation with as much enthusiasm as you can. Note how you feel.

➤ Do the exercise at least three times, recording yourself at least once at boredom, at a little bit of interest, at a lot of interest, and then at enthusiasm.

➤ Now listen to yourself. Note how you felt on each different time. Notice the difference between being bored and being enthusiastic.

➤ Finding your right vibration. For some, you might find that being enthusiastic right away just doesn't feel right. At first, you may find that you're most comfortable saying your affirmations with interest or even high interest. That's okay. What you want to do is work your way up to being enthusiastic. You will find as you have success with your affirmations, you will be able to say them with more and more enthusiasm. Up to that point, however, remember this truth: if you want to be enthusiastic, act enthusiastic.

➤ Say three of your favorite affirmations with the right vibration for you, at least three times during the day.

END-OF-THE-DAY POWER AFFIRMATION:

Say this with certainty: Congratulations (say your name or say self, whichever you're most comfortable with). I have just had a superb day with my affirmations program! My affirmations work. I feel awesome, able to create anything I desire. I am *unstoppable*.

The Decision Switch

*Belief consists in accepting the affirmations
of the soul; unbelief, in denying them.*
—Ralph Waldo Emerson

Thoughts take less than a second to complete. It takes me way longer to write "I'm thin," than it does to think it! But as you think, "I'm thin," and the mirror is telling you something different, you, in another instant think, "I'm fat." What do you do? You make the instant decision that no matter what the present moment is telling you, your affirmation is true. Who cares what the mirror gives back to you. Affirmations are about creating what you want, not keeping in place what you have—if what you have isn't the ideal scene!

Flip the decision switch and believe in what is possible, not what is. If you want to be a millionaire and your check-book balance is hovering around the red zone, just decide that you're in the black, that you have an abundance of money. Keep affirming what you want and sooner or later, you will get it!

Affirmation Action Step #9:

➤ What is it that your heart desires?

➤ Decide to have that—what "that" is. Don't pay attention to what the reality of the present moment is.

➤ Use the decision switch whenever you start having negative thoughts. Ladies, if you want to be a size ten, then decide to be a size ten and keep affirming that no matter what happens.

➤ No matter what you want, you have to decide to have it. So go ahead, decide, and then keep affirming that decision and taking action towards making it happen.

END-OF-THE-DAY POWER AFFIRMATION:

Say this with *passion*: Congratulations (say your name or say self, whichever you're most comfortable with). I just had a magnificent day with my affirmations program! My affirmations work. I feel awesome, able to create anything I desire. I am *unstoppable*.

New Day Affirmation

*If one advances confidently in the direction of
one's dreams, and endeavors to live the life
that one has imagined, one will meet with a
success unexpected in common hours.*

—Henry David Thoreau

The sun rises. It is a new day, full of glorious possibilities. You have the power to make anything you want happen in this new day. Because you get what you expect, why not start the day expecting great things to happen in your life right when you wake up in the morning?

This is one of Scott's favorite tools to give his clients. He has them do this step every morning, religiously. Those that do follow his advice find that it changes their attitude for the day. They started expecting great things to happen and so they do! The bottom line is you always get what you expect!

Affirmation Action Step #10:

➤ Write down on four different note cards the following affirmations:

✦ This is the beginning of a new day full of new opportunities and possibilities.

✦ I am thankful and grateful for this day.

✦ I know that life is planning to do me good today, and I am curious and cannot wait to see what it is.

✦ Something *great* is going to happen today!

➤ Memorize two of the above affirmations, the two that really resonate with you.

➤ Say this every morning as soon as you wake up.

➤ Make sure to say other affirmations throughout the day that target what you want to have success in.

END-OF-THE-DAY POWER AFFIRMATION:

Say this with *belief*: Congratulations (say your name or say self, whichever you're most comfortable with). I just had an enjoyable day with my affirmations program! My affirmations work. I feel awesome, able to create anything I desire. I am *unstoppable*.

Creative Bombardment

Constant repetition carries conviction.
—Robert Collier

This is a true story. There was a guy who owned his own business. It was doing okay but it wasn't really producing the profits that he wanted. He decided to do something about it; he bought an extra water heater. That might sound strange until you know that he also laminated his favorite financial and prosperity affirmations and hung them in the shower. The extra water heater provided him with a guaranteed twenty minute shower every morning, and so every morning for twenty minutes he said his affirmations. He was committed—he did this every day. Not only was he always squeaky clean, he programmed his whole being for success on a daily basis for twenty minutes. His company soon turned into a multimillion dollar organization, and he credits his twenty-minute affirmation shower for this success.[6]

You are starting to see how powerful affirmations really are when you say them everyday. Now, you need to bombard your mind. You need to paper your house with affirmations so that they are everywhere. You want to see them everywhere you look, so you are reminded to say them over and over and over.

Affirmation Action Step #11:

➤ Pick out your top five to ten affirmations.

➤ Get some colored construction paper and pick the appropriate colors. Here are the most popular.

- ✦ Green: abundance
- ✦ Red: action
- ✦ Yellow: heart warming
- ✦ Purple: success
- ✦ Blue: calming

➤ Write one affirmation in big bold letters on one piece of paper. (You could also make them big on your computer and then paste the affirmation onto the paper.)

➤ Tape them up all over your house and in your car. Put affirmations in your bedroom and in your bathroom, on your computer, your refrigerator and your bathroom mirror. Don't forget to put one or two or five in your shower. Put them in your wallet and/or purse so that you take them out and see them. Tape them on the dashboard of your car and on the visor—both sides. Think about where you spend time. If you cook, put affirmations on the wall above the counter where you do your prep work. If you spend time in your garage, put it on the wall behind your workbench. If you're in a tool box all day long, put them inside the lid so that every time you open your toolbox, you see it.

➤ As you go by any one of these affirmations, say it out loud with lots of enthusiasm.

END-OF-THE-DAY POWER AFFIRMATION:

Say this with *enthusiasm*: Congratulations (say your name or say self, whichever you're most comfortable with). I just had a spectacular day with my affirmations program! My affirmations work. I feel awesome, able to create anything I desire. I am *unstoppable*.

Quantum Leap Affirmations

First say to yourself what you would be;
and then do what you have to do.

—Epictetus

One of the best parts about doing affirmations daily is that they are the most effective way to get you through the quantum leap. In other words, they get you where you want to go *fast*.

You read about Tracy Repchuk's quantum leap in part two. Patricia's success editing for one of the fastest growing companies in the United States is another great example of quantum leaps. She and Scott met up at Christmas, 2006. By February, 2007, she was part of the company's list of editors, and by June she was writing and editing for high-end clients and commanding high percentages of the royalties from the books she helped edit and write. Now she even owns her own publishing company—Roberts & Ross.

A quantum leap is something that takes you from the beginning to the end of a task at an accelerated rate. With it, you skip the steps that you thought were necessary but slowing you down. It is something that can also take you farther than you expected!

Tracy Repchuk puts it this way: incremental steps are fine. Hard work, knocking off items on your to-do list, slowly but surely working your way towards your goals—that's all fine too. But what can happen when you only take the small steps? You can get bored, distracted, procrastinate, get frustrated, give up, need money now, can no longer wait, and jump from concept to concept looking for a quick way.

The quick way is the Quantum Leap way!

Tracy has a great way to get you making these Quantum Leaps. Here they are:

Affirmation Action Step #12:

➤ Write down one of your goals, one of the things you want to accomplish in your life.

➤ Make this goal a 'no matter what' goal by saying this affirmation:

✦ "I am doing _____ no matter what!" This statement makes this goal very important. (Make sure you write this down on a card and file it in your Affirmations Box.)

➤ Ask yourself a big question, like: "what do I need to do to make a quantum leap with what I'm working on?" This question will provide you with an answer that will put you in action.

➤ Plan for your quantum leap by first writing down your desired end point. It may seem out of your reach right now, but believe that this end point is possible.

➤ Decide to take massive action. From this point forward, you are deciding to put extra effort into your quantum leap goal item. From this point forward, you are going to do something towards this goal every day.

➤ Write the following affirmation on a card:

✦ I am what I want; I do what I want, and I have what I want, all as fast as I want.

➤ Say this affirmation one hundred times throughout the day.

For more quantum leap affirmations, please visit www.bestaffirmations.com.

END-OF-THE-DAY POWER AFFIRMATION:

Say this with *intention*: Congratulations (say your name or say self, whichever you're most comfortable with). I just had a fantastic day with my affirmations program! My affirmations work. I feel awesome, able to create anything I desire. I am *unstoppable*.

Get an Affirmation Buddy

*Coming together is a beginning; keeping together
is progress; working together is success.*
—Henry Ford

The idea for this day's task originated about three years ago when Scott and his good friend, Dr. Paul Gluch, started saying affirmations to each other as a way to start their phone calls. Now, Scott and Patricia do this as well, and inevitably it makes them laugh which, of course, raises their vibrations.

All great successes actually come when people help each other. Teamwork is vital to any success. Zig Ziglar has a great saying: "If you want to fly with the eagles, stop scratching with the turkeys. Get around people who will inspire you." There's actually an intriguing statistic that backs this up. If you take your five closest friends and average all of your incomes, the average income will usually be within $5,000 of each of your income.

Also, by finding and using an affirmation buddy, you're tapping into one of the other laws of physics: two entities together are stronger than they are if they acted individually.

Affirmation Action Step #13:

➤ Find someone you can share affirmations with. Pick someone with whom you talk everyday. They need to positive, enthusiastic, and share your belief in affirmations.

➤ Call this person three times today, beginning each call with an affirmation. Say it with as much enthusiasm and joy as you can.

➤ From this point forward, every time you call this person, begin the phone conversation with an affirmation. Have a list of your favorite affirmations by the phone so that you're ready when he or she calls you. Call this person sometimes just to give them the affirmation.

➤ Make sure that you also say your three most important affirmations at least three times each throughout the day.

END-OF-THE-DAY POWER AFFIRMATION:

Say this with *focus*: Congratulations (say your name or say self, whichever you're most comfortable with). I just had an incredible day with my affirmations program! My affirmations work. I feel awesome, able to create anything I desire. I am *unstoppable*.

Personalizing Your Affirmations

All the fun is in how you say a thing.
—Robert Frost

At the beginning of the program, we gave you a list of ten affirmations, and we had you add some as you've progressed through the program. The affirmations that we've given you are among the best. Some of them we've found in various places, others we made up ourselves. However, Affirmations are intensely personal statements. Today's task is to learn how to personalize them (if you haven't done so already!).

Personalizing your affirmations helps make them really resonate with you. When you personalize an affirmation, you can make it align, deeply, with your belief system and your values. The stronger the connection with the affirmation, the deeper the impression it makes on you as a being, the more you believe it, and the more it works.

Sometimes, all you need to do is change one word to make the affirmation work better for you. For example, Patricia loves the affirmation "money flows to me easily and effortlessly." However, she changed it to "money flows to me easily, effortlessly, and abundantly," because she was getting money flows with the first one, but they weren't large enough. Once she added "abundantly," then the $350 she would get consistently changed into $1000 to $1500 consistently.

Affirmation Action Step #14:

➤ Find an affirmation that you like but you've never felt that it is quite right.

➤ Re-word the affirmation so that it fits your personality. Sometimes people find that affirmations are too straightforward. Some people like to add expressions of gratitude to the affirmation, or you can re-word them to match your values and even your spiritual beliefs. For example, if "I have wealth and prosperity" is too absolute, try "I am grateful for my wealth and prosperity," or "I am comfortable with the thought of my income exceeding my expenses."

➤ Sometimes, as Patricia found, the affirmation you're working with isn't actually strong enough, does not affirm enough action, or doesn't say that the action is happening as fast as you want. Sometimes, all you have to do is put the word "now" in, and you're good to go.

➤ Sometimes, there might be a word that you need to take out. Take the affirmation that we gave you on Day Two: "Making money excites me and energizes me." A version of this affirmation read "making money juices me, excites me, and energizes me." We took the word "juices" out because we weren't sure if that would communicate to the majority of our readers. If it does, add it back in. But, the point of this suggestion is that you can change words, take them out, add them. Do what you need to do to get your affirmations resonating with your beliefs—with you! —so that they have as much power as they can.

➤ Take at least three more of your affirmations and personalize them.

Now, say these personalized affirmations at least three times each throughout the day.

END-OF-THE-DAY POWER AFFIRMATION:

Say this with *a feeling of persistence*: Congratulations (say your name or say self, whichever you're most comfortable with). I just had a phenomenal day with my affirmations program! My affirmations work. I feel awesome, able to create anything I desire. I am *unstoppable.*

The Principle of the Dominant Thought

*Whether you believe if you can do a thing
or not, you are correct.*

—Henry Ford

In part two, we talked about the fact that you have roughly fifty thousand thoughts per day, and studies have shown that for most people, 80 percent of these thoughts are negative. To make matters worse, the following day, 90 percent of your thoughts are the ones that you had the previous day. This is to remind you that you have habitual ways of thinking.

These habitual ways of thinking are apparent, sometimes glaringly so, all around you. If life isn't going well, your habitual thoughts are probably negative.

The Principle of the Dominant Thought is to get you to look. Look at what is happening in your life. Is it going the way that you want? Are you still concentrating on your bills, on not having enough money? Is life still too overwhelming because you don't have enough time?

By simply stepping back and observing, you can spot an amazing amount of things. You can actually spot the fact that because you are concentrating on how many bills you have and how much money you spend paying them, then your bills are still hounding you. Abundance is not happening. Or, if you don't have enough time, is it because you're constantly saying: "I don't have enough time?" That's your dominant thought, and whatever you're thinking is manifesting. It's that simple.

To change it, all you have to do is look at what isn't working and do the following to turn it around.

Affirmation Action Step #15:

➤ Take a moment and just look at your life. What is working and what isn't working. Simply take a look at what isn't working.

➤ Once you have located the trouble spot, look at your dominant thought about that area. If you're having trouble sleeping is it because you constantly say: "I don't sleep well"?

➤ Usually the dominant thoughts that get you into trouble begin with "I don't."

➤ List out all the "I don't" thoughts that you have about your trouble area. If you find other "I don't" thoughts in other areas, write them down too.

➤ Now, you need to change these dominant "I don't" thoughts into positive statements. If your dominant thought is "I don't have enough money," change it to "I have plenty of money."

➤ Make sure that the change you make puts your new affirmation in positive, active terms. This is key: make sure that they are always in present tense, never in future tense. (You'll get this information again in a few days when you actually make your own affirmations.) For example, it doesn't work to say, "I will be a success," because you're affirming that your success is going to happen someday in the future. But you see, that future is always going to remain in the future. It never will happen in the present. So instead, say "I am a success now."

The most important point: if you focus on debt, you're going to get more of it. Focus on positive things, and positive things will start happening. Remember the Law of Attraction? This is simply another formulation of it. Like attracts like. Be aware of what you're thinking, but instead of beating yourself up about thinking negatively, just simply change your thoughts to the positive.

END-OF-THE-DAY POWER AFFIRMATION:

Say this with *conviction*: Congratulations (say your name or say self, whichever you're most comfortable with). I just had a marvelous day with my affirmations program! My affirmations work. I feel awesome, able to create anything I desire. I am *unstoppable*.

Your Morning Pep Rally

*When you are inspired by some great purpose, some
extraordinary project, all your thoughts break their
bounds: your mind transcends limitations, your
consciousness expands in every direction and you
find yourself in a new, great and wonderful world.
Dormant forces, faculties and talents become alive,
and you discover yourself to be a greater person by
far than you ever dreamed yourself to be.*

—Patanjali

What happens when you get excited at a sports event?
You jump up and down, lock your elbows in victory,
and shout for joy, all in total enthusiasm. And you feel
great! Why? Because your vibration is as high as it can be.

This is what you want to capture with affirmations. You
want to have a pep rally every morning and shout, squeal,

and howl your affirmations. Patricia does it with her young daughter every morning and the little one loves it. She jumps up and down, yelling "woo-hoo"—sort of—and gets her plump little arms waving up and down. It's not only the most adorable thing on the planet; it also helps to raise the vibration level even higher. And, you guessed it, everything that Patricia affirms in her morning pep rally happens, and it happens fast.

Affirmation Action Step #16:

➤ Right now, think of one thing that you want to have happen today. Do you want to close three new clients? Do you need to make $3,000 today? Whatever it is, start having your very own pep rally. Jump up and down, dance around, laugh, and yell as loudly as you can, "I closed three new clients today." Then give a "woo-hoo" or an "all right," or even an "I did it!" and keep dancing and jumping and shouting affirmations.

Do this for at least one minute. If you're having fun, don't stop! Do it until your vibration level is at an all time high. Then, get to work and see what happens!

END-OF-THE-DAY POWER AFFIRMATION:

Say this with *confidence*: Congratulations (say your name or say self, whichever you're most comfortable with). I just had a fabulous day with my affirmations program! My affirmations work. I feel awesome, able to create anything I desire. I am *unstoppable*.

Visualizing Your Affirmations as Real

Formulate and stamp indelibly on your mind a mental picture of yourself as succeeding. Hold this picture tenaciously. Never permit it to fade. Your mind will seek to develop the picture.

—Norman Vincent Peale

Visualization is a more in-depth way in which to make your thoughts more powerful. Visualization is giving substance to your thoughts. The visualization process is a whole art unto itself, and our next handbook will deal with that aspect. To get affirmations to do what you want them to do, you need to really get a strong mental picture of what it looks like to have your affirmations coming true. If you have been affirming that you are healthy, wealthy, thin, and happy, get the picture of you really being healthy, wealthy, thin, and happy.

Scott has a great visualization exercise designed to get you really picturing what it looks like when your affirmations have come true. At one point, he had to actually stop doing this everyday because he had so much business that he had to make sure that he could fully deliver what he had promised! He also has a great story about a client of his in the U. K. who used visualization. This client wanted his mortgage to be paid off; it was one of his big goals. So Scott had him visualize his mortgage being paid off, and this client did this every day. Within two years, his mortgage was paid! (And the next month he and his wife bought a Mercedes Benz with the money they didn't have to spend on the mortgage!!)

Affirmation Action Step #17:

➤ Get into a quiet place. Close your eyes and take a couple of deep breaths. Start smiling.

➤ Take one of your affirmations. Say the affirmation with total belief and then start to see yourself exactly how you will be when that affirmation happens. For example, if your affirmation is "I am financially free," then see yourself being totally financially free. What does it look like and feel like?

➤ Now, start really getting a great picture of you having your affirmations come true. Get the full picture, the sights and sounds, how it feels on the inside to have this come true. Use all of your senses and make a movie of it.

➤ Have fun with this. There's an old saying in the self-help circles: All great successes start with a mental picture of you succeeding.

END-OF-THE-DAY POWER AFFIRMATION:

Say this with *certainty*: Congratulations (say your name or say self, whichever you're most comfortable with). I just had a sensational day with my affirmations program! My affirmations work. I feel awesome, able to create anything I desire. I am *unstoppable*.

Reflection Day

The unexamined life is not worth living.
—Socrates

Congratulations! You have learned eighteen different strategies for using affirmations! We sincerely hope that some of these tools not only have helped you to change your mindset, but have blown your socks off!

With all this affirming, I'm sure things are happening. So today's tool is a day for reflection, to step back and take note of what has been happening in your life since you started this program. You want to look at what worked for you and what didn't so that as you move forward with your affirmations, you can be even more aware of their power and what you need to do to make them more effective!

Affirmation Action Step #18:

➤ Pick out the one day that you felt had the biggest impact on you.

➤ Do that step again today.

➤ Now, spend some time thinking and even writing on these questions. You don't have to answer them all, just the ones that really trigger thoughts:

✦ What are the three best things that happened to you today?

✦ What are you most grateful for?

✦ Do you feel any differently now than you did yesterday?

✦ Did anything fun or important or unexpected happen today?

✦ Did this exercise help you to really pack more power into your affirmations?

➤ Other questions that help the reflection process include:

✦ How do you feel about life in general?

✦ How do you feel your thought patterns have changed?

✦ Are you getting up differently or going to bed differently?

✦ Have your dreams changed?

✦ Have you had any major successes happen? What are they?

✦ How did you feel when it happened?

+ Are you taking more action? Are you enjoying the process?
+ Are you enjoying life more?
+ Are you becoming your own best friend?

Whatever triggers you to reflect, go for it! The most important point is that you take a look backward so that you can continue moving forward.

END-OF-THE-DAY POWER AFFIRMATION:

Say this with *passion*: Congratulations (say your name or say self, whichever you're most comfortable with). I just had a great day with my affirmations program! My affirmations work. I feel awesome, able to create anything I desire. I am *unstoppable*.

P.S.: If you find that you're getting bogged down and that you're not progressing as well as you like, we understand. We have a five-star coaching program available to you. We will hold you accountable through each step, and we will add more personal touches to help you take your career, your life, and/or your business to the next level. If you're interested in live coaching, visit us at www.bestaffirmationscoach.com.

Flip Switching the Negative to the Positive

Formulate and stamp indelibly on your mind a mental picture of yourself as succeeding. Hold this picture tenaciously. Never permit it to fade. Your mind will seek to develop the picture.

—Norman Vincent Peale

We haven't looked at negativity in a while, and because it sometimes pops up when things are going really, really well, here's another great way to handle it. It's sort of the "flip" side to the decision switch.

Dr. Robert Anthony is an expert in helping people change their vibrations from negative to positive. We all know that it is important to "think positive," but when you have fifty thousand or so thoughts a day, sometimes that is hard to do. The negative thoughts happen in a moment and if you're not prepared, they can ruin your day (or the rest of your life, if you don't change them to the positive). Dr. Anthony recognized that in order to "think positive" it is vital to have an affirmation always handy, always ready, so that when those pesky moments of negativity pop up, you can simply "flip the switch."

Here's what you do. When you become aware of a negative thought or emotion, you simply and powerfully 'flip the switch.' In that moment of negativity, you simply think positive. You say an affirmation.

Patricia does it this way. "When I find myself dwelling on how much I owe on my energy bill or how much diapers cost, I stop the negative thought and immediately think, 'Money flows freely and effortlessly in my universe,' or, 'I have great abundance in my life.' I have my favorite financial abundance affirmations memorized and ready to go so when I 'flip switch' I can do it fast and effortlessly. And I repeat that affirmation until I feel the negativity just flow away. It's magic."

Affirmation Action Step #19:

➤ Get your favorite affirmations ready. Memorize two.

➤ Practice the flip switching technique. Pretend that you're having a negative thought and the moment you realize it, say an affirmation and hold the positive thought for fifteen seconds.

➤ Now, throughout the day, the second you feel a negative thought or feeling coming on, have your affirmation ready. Say it out loud. Make yourself smile when you say it. Shout it, if you need to. Then, make sure you hold the positive thought for fifteen seconds. Do whatever is necessary to flip the negative to the positive. When you feel the positive vibration flowing through you and around you, then you have successfully flipped your switch from positive to negative.

END-OF-THE-DAY POWER AFFIRMATION:

Say this with *belief*: Congratulations (say your name or say self, whichever you're most comfortable with). I just had a super day with my affirmations program! My affirmations work. I feel awesome, able to create anything I desire. I am *unstoppable*.

The Power of Laughter

*Laugh and your life will be lengthened for
this is the great secret of long life.*
—Og Mandino

If you think smiling is powerful, wait until you try laughing! Laughter is one of the most joyous, delightful and powerful ways to raise your vibration. Norman Cousins recognized the power of laughter in his book on illness. Laughter helps you get better because it raises your vibrations.

Sometimes, you might not feel like laughing. That is understandable, but what we're going for here is you tapping into your power to create anything you want, and that includes emotions. If you make yourself laugh, you might actually find that there are plenty of things to laugh about!

Affirmation Action Step #20:

➤ Get your favorite affirmation from the box, or if you want to try a new one, go to your favorite affirmations source on the web or visit our www.bestaffirmations.com site. We want you to get the affirmation that really says what you want it to say.

➤ Read the affirmation out loud and start laughing. Really get a good laugh going, then when you're feeling really good, shout your affirmation. Laugh as you say it. Find some other affirmations that you want to say. Laugh and say those. Feel the happiness inside you as you really feel your vibration go up.

➤ If you need some help laughing, do this:

Write down the five funniest things that happened to you. This will get you in the vibration of create.

- Or -

Call the funniest person you know, someone who makes you laugh. Just laugh and laugh as much as you can. This raises your vibrations, so that when you say your affirmations, you are saying them in a fun, clean space and your message is clear.

END-OF-THE-DAY POWER AFFIRMATION:

Say this with *intention*: Congratulations (say your name or say self, whichever you're most comfortable with). I just had a brilliant day with my affirmations program! My affirmations work. I feel awesome, able to create anything I desire. I am *unstoppable*.

Affirmations for Gratitude

At times our own light goes out and is rekindled by a spark from another person. Each of us has cause to think with deep gratitude of those who have lighted the flame within us.

—Albert Schweitzer

There is another law of the universe that you want to tap into. It is the law of gratitude. We have found this to be true over and over. When you are grateful, you will attract more things to be grateful for, and when you are grateful you are truly rich. Sir John Templeton, a very wealthy man, said it best: when you are grateful for all the things in your life, you will have more things in your life to be grateful for.

When you are grateful, you are open to receiving. Your vibrations are high. You are able to accept good things. One of our favorite clients is one of the most grateful people we know. She has such a strong sense of gratitude that she attracts amazing people and things in her life. She's writing a book; her business is booming, and she's really starting to live the life she's always wanted to. She's unstoppable, and it's because she is always so grateful for what she has and what she is able to create.

Affirmation Action Step #21:

➤ Write down the following affirmations on note cards:

- ✦ Gratitude and I are one.

- ✦ I am grateful for all the things in my life.

- ✦ My attitude of gratitude makes me a wealthy individual.

➤ Write down at least ten things that you are grateful for.

➤ Pick your favorite gratitude affirmation and say it with feeling at least five times as you have your ten items in mind.

END-OF-THE-DAY POWER AFFIRMATION:

Say this with *focus*: Congratulations (say your name or say self, whichever you're most comfortable with). I just had a top-notch day with my affirmations program! My affirmations work. I feel awesome, able to create anything I desire. I am *unstoppable*.

Take an Affirmation Walk

*In every walk with nature, one
receives far more than he seeks.*

—John Muir

Sometimes during the day, you get bogged down. You've been inside working on your computer all day. You're tired because your dog or your kid or your husband or wife kept you up. Life just seems to be dragging, and sometimes that can pull in a lot of negativity. And because you're feeling overwhelmed by it all, the negativity is getting you down and nothing seems to be working to bring it all back to the positive.

At this point, the best thing for you to do is take an Affirmation Walk. Walking is great because it not only gets your blood moving which gets oxygen flowing in your body which in turn makes you feel physically better, it also gets your attention directed in the right direction. Walking turns you from looking inward, which is negative, to outward, which is positive. The important point to walking is that you look at things, be aware of all that is around you. Feel the air on your face, the sun warming your skin. Watch the birds fly over and the trees moving in the wind. Marvel at the beauty of a flower. All of these things gently bring you back into a positive space so that you're able to get on with your day.

Affirmation Action Step #22:

➤ Even though you might not be feeling bogged today, your action step is to go for an Affirmation Walk to get the idea of how it works.

➤ As you walk, look at things. Think of it as a great way to get connected back to nature. Bring gratitude into it. Be glad that you are part of this great, beautiful world. Then, as you walk, say your favorite affirmations. Say them out loud if you're comfortable with doing that. Walk with passion and purpose, and have a big smile on your face, so that everyone who sees you thinks: I want some of what that person has!

All of our clients learn how to take an Affirmation Walk. It is a staple in handling those times when all seems dark. Countless clients tell us how a simple walks lifts their spirits and they feel ready, willing, and able to start creating again.

END-OF-THE-DAY POWER AFFIRMATION:

Say this with *a feeling of persistence*: Congratulations (say your name or say self, whichever you're most comfortable with). I just had a miraculous day with my affirmations program! I feel awesome, able to create anything I desire. My affirmations work. I am *unstoppable*.

Handling the Night Sweats

> *The more tranquil a man becomes, the greater is his success, his influence, his power for good. Calmness of mind is one of the beautiful jewels of wisdom.*
> —James Allen

Have you ever had this, or some version of it, happen to you? You're sound asleep, but all of a sudden, you wake up in the middle of the night, heart pounding and palms sweating. You can't stop thinking about what you don't have or what you haven't done. And the rudest part of the whole thing is you can't get back to sleep for awhile. This might not happen to everyone, but we have found that it is prevalent enough in our clients that we want to address it here.

There are millions of different things that can keep a person awake at night—while money worries seem to top the list, it might be caused by the presentation you have to give at work the next day, the report that you have to write, or even the sink that you have to fix. Whatever the case, the underlying cause is that the dominant thought that you have about your item of worry is negative.

This used to happen to Patricia frequently, until she discovered affirmations. Here is what she does to handle her 3:00 a. m. insomnia sessions:

Affirmation Action Step #23:

➤ Identify the area that is causing the problem. This is the thing that you can't get your mind off of, the one that you go over and over in your head while you're trying to go back to sleep.

➤ Write down all the affirmations you can think of that puts that area into a positive light. Writing them down is really important. It has a wonderfully calming effect.

➤ When you're back in bed, lying down, get in the most comfortable position you can find and say to yourself: "I am asleep," over and over until you fall asleep!

Another affirmation that works well for sleep is: "I sleep well so that I wake up refreshed and energized."

END-OF-THE-DAY POWER AFFIRMATION:

Say this with *confidence*: Congratulations (say your name or say self, whichever you're most comfortable with). I just had a wondrous day with my affirmations program! My affirmations work. I feel awesome, able to create anything I desire. I am *unstoppable*.

Practice Writing Your Own Affirmations

*Each thought that is welcomed and recorded is a
nest egg by the side of which more will be laid.*
—Henry David Thoreau

Many coaches insist that the best affirmations are the ones that you make because you know best what you want to have happen. We find that as long as the affirmations you are saying resonate with you, then they work. It doesn't really matter if they are yours or if someone gave them to you.

However, it is very handy to know how to make your own affirmations because there are going to be situations in your life that are highly specific to you and where you need an affirmation. Say for example, you want to keep your house tidier but you just can't seem to make that happen. You can make an affirmation to help you get into the right mindset of a tidy house. You can simply say: "My house is always tidy," or "I like keeping my house tidy." The possibilities for affirmations are endless. It all depends on what you want to change or to improve in your life.

There's also an added bonus to doing this: knowing how to create your own affirmations can also help you when you have those moments of doubt and negativity and you don't have an affirmation ready to say.

To create your own affirmations, there are a few important points that you need to follow to make them effective:

➤ State them in present tense. We talked about this on Day 15—Observing What is Happening—but it is so important that it's worth repeating. Your thoughts create the things that you want to happen. If you say an affirmation in future tense, "I will," or "It will," then you're creating something in a future that is always going to stay in the future.

It will never come true in any present moment that you are living. It's a little bit like a mind trick. You make your affirmations in the present because at some point you want them to happen in the present. You are creating a future present by saying your affirmations in the present tense. Here's an example: "I have an abundance of joy, success, and wealth *now*." Now is this true in that first moment that you say it? Probably not. But, when you keep saying it, at some point that "now" is going to happen, and then your affirmation will be true.

➤ Affirmations express a positive statement. Always state affirmations in the most positive way that you can. Affirm what you do want rather than what you don't want. Keep all negativity out of the affirmations. For example, many of our clients don't want to worry about bills. We can understand that, but bills are negative, so you don't want your affirmation to read: "I do not have any bills." That is actually reinforcing part of the negativity. The trick here is to find the real negative behind the problem and then look at what it's true opposite is. Not being able to pay bills means that you don't have enough money. That's the real negative at work here. But not having enough money is easily turned around into having enough money. So the affirmation to cover your desire to not have any bills is "My life is filled with an abundance of wealth, now!"

➤ They are short statements. If affirmations get too long, then they don't pack as much punch. Short statements are easy to say, easy to remember, and they send a powerful message to the universe that you mean business about what you say!

➤ They use active words: "have," "do" "filled." There is nothing wrong with saying "My life is a masterpiece," but you don't want all of your affirmations to have as their only action word "am" "is" and "are." You want to use phrases like "I accomplish...," "I have...," "I use...," "My life is now filled...," etc. One way to find the right action words is to look over a list of affirmations and see what words they use.

➤ Finally, a great way to make your own affirmations is do what you did on Day 15, look for your dominant thought. If that thought is negative, change it to the positive.

Here are some great ways to start affirmations:

    I am…

    I have…

    My life is now filled…

    I experience…

    I use…

    I feel…

    I deserve…

    I expect…

Here are some expressions to stay away from:

    I hope…

    I might…

    I could…

    I should…

    I don't…

Affirmation Action Step #24:

➤ Find an area of your life that you want to change.

➤ Find the real negative in what is going on.

➤ Write three affirmations that help you handle that aspect.

➤ Do this three more times.

END-OF-THE-DAY POWER AFFIRMATION:

Say this with *confidence*: Congratulations (say your name or say self, whichever you're most comfortable with). I have had a stupendous day with my affirmations program! My affirmations work. I feel awesome, able to create anything I desire. I am *unstoppable*.

Belief

Believe it can be done. When you believe something can be done, really believe, your mind will find the ways to do it. Believing a solution paves the way to a solution.

—David J. Schwartz

Belief is another cornerstone to affirmations. You must believe in your affirmations in order for them to work. Remember, saying one affirmation with belief is more powerful than saying 100 of the same affirmations with no belief.

Early on, we had you affirming that your affirmations work. This is a companion exercise. What you believe is what you will manifest in your life. When you first started out, you had to really mock up believing that the affirmations you were saying were true. Now, with only six days left of this program, we hope that you are finding that it is becoming easier and easier to believe your affirmations because you are having more and greater successes with them.

We see this happening over and over. Just recently, Scott had a potential new client call. Like many of Scott's other clients, he was having trouble getting his affirmations to work. Scott immediately identified the problem—this gentleman didn't believe that they would work. Once Scott pointed this out, the potential new client knew immediately that Scott was right. The gentleman is now Scott's client and his affirmations stick because he believes in them!

Affirmation Action Step #25:

➤ Say this affirmation:

I have absolute certainty, confidence, and belief that my affirmations work.

➤ Say this one hundred times, either all at once or throughout the day, and as you say it, feel with every fiber of your being and every cell of your body, believe that it will work.

Get to the point where you are saying it with total belief that it will work.

Remember, when you believe, you achieve. The size of your success is determined by the size of your belief. Believe and achieve!

END-OF-THE-DAY POWER AFFIRMATION:

Say this with *certainty*: Congratulations (say your name or say self, whichever you're most comfortable with). I just had a glorious day with my affirmations program! I feel awesome, able to create anything I desire. I am *unstoppable*.

Persistence

Nothing in this world can take the place of persist-
ence. Talent will not; nothing is more common
than unsuccessful people with talent. Genius will
not; unrewarded genius is almost a proverb.
Education will not; the world is full of educated
derelicts. Persistence and determination alone are
omnipotent. The slogan "press on" has solved and
always will solve the problems of the human race.

—Calvin Coolidge

Old Calvin Coolidge is so right. Persistence is the back-bone to making anything happen. Bernard Percy, parenting coach and award-winning author, has this on his business card: Everything turns out right in the end; if it isn't right...it isn't the end! Anyone who has succeeded in his or her life knows the truth of this. You only are done when everything has turned out like you want it to!

There are hundreds and hundreds of stories that give testament to the power of persistence. Scott's book *Boston Marathon or Bust* (www.bostonmarathonorbust.com) talks about how it took him twelve years and twelve marathons to qualify for the Boston Marathon. He did it because he hired a coach, was persistent and used whatever tools he had to get there. He considers it one of his greatest achievements. For those who succeed, they know that it takes the attitude of "never give up."

The whole point to this day is for you to really understand that this is what you have been doing all the time. Affirmations are beliefs, and to make a belief real, you have to be persistent.

Affirmation Action Step #26:

➤ This is familiar, but we're having you do it do make a point. Take your favorite affirmation and say it one hundred times. Repetition is the mother of skill, but rather than saying it throughout the day, persist until you have said it one hundred times!

➤ Decide that from this day forward, you are going to say your affirmations every day and all the time.

➤ Then, throughout the rest of this day, throughout the day, say this at least ten times: "Everyday, in everyway, I get better and better."

END-OF-THE-DAY POWER AFFIRMATION:

Say this with *passion*: Congratulations (say your name or say self, whichever you're most comfortable with). I just had a super day with my affirmations program! My affirmations work. I feel awesome, able to create anything I desire. I am *unstoppable.*

Listening to Your Affirmations

It's the repetition of affirmations that leads to belief. And once that belief becomes a deep conviction, things begin to happen.
—Claude M. Bristol

One powerful way to keep your affirmations constantly in the forefront of your mind is to record them and then listen to them throughout the day. Listening to affirmations is almost as powerful as saying them, and by listening to them, they keep you in a positive mindset.

One of Scott's clients had a terrible fear of public speaking. Like the majority of people, it was one of her biggest fears. She recorded her affirmations on public speaking and then listened to them on a regular basis. Within a year she was giving speeches at Toastmasters and felt great. Just recently, she became President of her local Toastmasters club!

Affirmation Action Step #27:

➤ Gather your favorite and most powerful affirmations. These can be those we gave you, those you found on the internet, or those you made yourself.

➤ Record them on a cassette player or an iPod. (If you don't own either one, you can purchase an inexpensive cassette player at most big box retailers.) As an alternative, you can also download the audio affirmations we have on our website: www.bestaffirmations.com. Your own voice is best, but if this is easier for you, that's fine.

➤ Record your affirmations using "I," and then record them using your name. For example: "I create wealth easily and effortlessly," and then "Scott creates wealth easily and effortlessly." This is a form of creative bombardment. Hearing your name actually jolts you out of your complacency of thinking of yourself as an "I." Try it and you'll see what we mean.

➤ Listen to these affirmations throughout the day, when you're on your Affirmations Walk, when you're doing yard work or cleaning house. Listen to them when you have a moment of down time at work (but we're not advising you to listen to your affirmations instead of work!) Find time to listen to them throughout the day.

➤ If you have the right equipment, put on your headphones and listen to your affirmations right before you go to sleep. This is a powerful way to keep yourself plugged into the positive.

END-OF-THE-DAY POWER AFFIRMATION:

Say this with *belief*: Congratulations (say your name or say self, whichever you're most comfortable with). I just had a nifty day with my affirmations program! My affirmations work. I feel awesome, able to create anything I desire. I am *unstoppable*.

Become an Island of Positive Vibrations

*Offer a vibration that matches your
desire rather than offering a vibration
that keeps matching what is.*
—Abraham Hicks

Negativity is all around us. We hear it on the news, read it in the papers, and we are bombarded with it from our co-workers. In order to keep yourself positive, you need to become an island of positive vibration. You want to get rid of the negative as much as possible, and you want to surround yourself with so much positive that the negative doesn't affect you.

Affirmation Action Step #28:

➤ Do not watch TV, listen to the radio, or read the newspaper. These are all full of negative news, and by reading about all the negatives it can bring you down.

➤ Concentrate on the positive. Look at your affirmations pasted up around your house. Listen to your affirmations. Listen to uplifting music or a great self-help CD like *The Secret*.

➤ Write down the following on cards:

✦ I am positive.

✦ My life is filled with positive thoughts.

✦ Good, positive things happen to me.

✦ I am an island of positive vibration.

➤ Pick your two favorites and say them as many times as you can throughout the day.

➤ File your cards at the end of the day.

Work to keep a constant flow of positive vibrations around you. When you do, the negativity stays out!

END-OF-THE-DAY POWER AFFIRMATION:

Say this with *enthusiasm*: Congratulations (say your name or say self, whichever you're most comfortable with). I just had a first-class day with my affirmations program! My affirmations work. I feel awesome, able to create anything I desire. I am *unstoppable*.

Deciding What Works Best for You

*If you have built castles in the air, your work
need not be lost; that is where they should be.
Now put the foundations under them.*

—Henry David Thoreau

Yου're almost done! You have one more day to go
before the celebration begins!

We've given you twenty-eight different tools to help you
really activate the power of affirmations. If you use just one
or two of them, we know that your life will never be the
same. But, we want you to spend today reflecting on what
worked best for you. Was it affirming that your affirmations
worked? Or was it changing your dominant thought?

Also, we have directed you to say your affirmations throughout the day, but we have found that most people find that they have a favorite time to say them. Some say them in the morning and at night. Some say them while they are getting ready for work or school. Some like to say their affirmations while they are cooking dinner or cleaning up afterwards.

Now that you have a feel for the whole thing, you need to pick your best time and place to do your affirmations and then resolve to do them at that time everyday.

Affirmation Action Step #29:

➤ Pick your best time to do your affirmations. (We highly recommend having first thing in the morning and last thing at night on your list.)

➤ Pick your best place to say them.

➤ Pick your best affirmations action step.

➤ Pick your best way to handle negativity.

➤ Decide that you are going to do your affirmations at this time, in this place, in this way, every day, no matter what.

➤ And, of course, always have affirmations ready so when negative thoughts creep in, you can change them to positive ones!

➤ If you're saying: "but I liked everything," *great*! Simply know that these are all tools for you to use when you need and want them. Also, be flexible. If a situation really calls for "flip-switching," or "observing what is happening," then use it!

It all really comes down to intention. You put in your intention into making yourself a success, and you will be a success. Affirmations take their power from intention. You cannot start anything or complete anything unless you have the intention to do so.

Get your intention in, and see where your life will go when you have the power to create the life that you want!

END-OF-THE-DAY POWER AFFIRMATION:

Say this with *belief*: Congratulations (say your name or say "self", whichever you're most comfortable with). I just had an astounding day with my affirmations program! I feel awesome, able to create anything I desire. I am *unstoppable*.

Celebrate Your Successes!

The more you praise and celebrate your life, the more there is in life to celebrate.

—Oprah Winfrey

Congratulations! You are actually part of a very small percentage of the population that has been able to follow through to the end of something like this. We salute you!! Go out and celebrate. Take yourself out to dinner, buy yourself a treat. Whatever works for you, do it because it is the vital last step—celebrate your success.

Also, in all the fun of celebrating, we want you to take some time and reflect on all that you have done and all that has happened to you as you went through this program.

Affirmation Action Step #30:

➤ Go back to the first day. There you will find two pieces of information. The first is "where would you like to be emotionally, physically, mentally, and spiritually." The second is the goal that you made for this program.

➤ Look at where you are now and how close you came to accomplishing those goals. Spend some time reflecting and writing on these questions: Did you come close to making your goal or did you surpass it? Did other unexpected yet highly desirable things happen because of this program? What do you think that you did to make these things happen?

➤ Look back over all the work you did as you learned the tools outlined in this handbook. Spend some time reflecting on and writing down all your successes, how you felt going through the program, and how you feel now that you finished. Reflect some more about the unexpected things that happened. Perhaps you were concentrating on financial abundance, but you found that your relationship with your partner or your children got better.

We hope that you found that your life took quantum leaps into both expected and unexpected places!!

END-OF-THE-DAY POWER AFFIRMATION:

Say this with *enthusiasm, intention, focus, a feeling of persistence, convictions, confidence, certainty, passion, and belief:* Congratulations (say your name or say self, whichever you're most comfortable with). I have just finished my affirmation program! My affirmations work. I feel awesome. I *am* able to create anything I desire. I am *unstoppable*.

Epilogue

*Charge your future! As you recreate this
positive force in your life, take big, massive
leaps into your future. Be imaginative, bold
and brave! The results may surprise you.*

—Jim Allen

Affirmations are a habit, and we hope that by getting to
this point, you have created a life-long habit. You are
now able to create anything that you want. You have the
power of the law of attraction firmly on your side. The
only way that you will lose that power is if you stop doing
your affirmations everyday.

Because really, this is not the end, it is just the beginning!
You now have so many tools, so many ways to manifest
abundance and goodness and health in your life.

Have the intention to continue doing affirmations
everyday and all the time. Play. Have fun creating. Yes,

you will run into days when things aren't working. That's when you go back to your program. Also, don't force things. One of Scott's favorite sayings is "Stop swimming upstream, just flow with the river." You might want something to happen, and you want it to happen fast, but it just isn't working out the way you want. That might be for a reason, and just know that if you want something to happen, keep affirming that it has already happened, and soon it will actually have happened.

And remember. Always, handle negativity with positive vibrations. It's really the only sane way to do things.

The best part about this handbook is, nothing's stopping you from picking an area of your life that you want to improve and taking another read through the book. You have the best tools that we know of that you can apply easily to any specific area in your life

One final note: as we have said over and over throughout this whole handbook, the best compliment that you can give us is by sharing this handbook with another person. As Harvey Firestone said: "It is only as we develop others that we permanently succeed." We really are committed to making this world a better place. It's why we started our Affirmations for Africa Foundation (www.AffirmationsforAfrica.com) and it's why we encourage you to share with others all these new tools that you have learned to use.

"Giving starts the receiving process," is one of our mottos. Give, and see what starts coming your way.

Again, very well done on getting
to this point!

We wish you all the success, joy, and
abundance that you can create!

Dr. Patricia Ross

Scott Sharp Armstrong

About the Authors

Scott Armstrong

Scott Armstrong has over twenty successful years of sales, marketing and personal development experience, bringing in millions of dollars of revenue.

Having himself been mentored by some of the world's best personal development teachers, such as Jim Rohn, Wayne Dyer, Tom Hopkins, Zig Ziglar, Brian Tracy, and Mike Litman, he's also participated in many of their motivational seminars around the country.

According to Scott, his most influential and life changing event was a four day seminar with Anthony Robbins concluding with the fire-walk experience. Completing the Robbins program helped him raise his "mental game" to an entirely new level!

Other lifetime achievements which helped instill him with lessons in teamwork, self-confidence, success principles, persistence and leadership include becoming an Eagle Scout at a young age, graduating from the University of Colorado, authoring a book, serving two terms as President of Toastmasters International, qualifying for and finishing the one hundredth running of the Boston Marathon and completing twelve additional marathons overall. He values his Boston Marathon achievement as one of his greatest personal success stories, incorporating some of the story into his motivational book, *Boston Marathon or Bust: How to Achieve Your Life, Sports, and Business Goals in Record Time.*

Being active and having accomplished so much in his life, Scott now has the inspiration, confidence and desire to motivate and teach others to achieve their goals and dreams. Scott's personal mission is to embody and promote all aspects of a healthy life—mental, emotional, physical and spiritual, while coaching people who are seeking success in areas related to personal development.

With that goal in mind, he has coached clients worldwide – from the United States, Canada, England, Ireland, Australia and New Zealand, to Switzerland, Sweden, South Africa, Denmark, Iceland, Czechoslovakia, Trinidad, and Curacao—sharing his secrets of success while encouraging his clients to achieve their own outstanding outcomes.

Scott lives with his beautiful wife Sarah, lakeside in the foothills of Boulder, Colorado, where he also bases Boulder Coaching Academy (www.BoulderCoachingAcademy.com). He encourages you to e-mail him with your questions at info@bestaffirmations.com.

Dr. Patricia Ross

Dr. Patricia Ross has been mentoring and coaching people from all walks of life for over fourteen years. She has attended and taught at some of the top universities in the country and was awarded her Ph. D. from New York University in 2004.

She began her career teaching college-level English, and she was dedicated to being one of the best university professors around. However, she quickly found that her students needed more help helping themselves be successful by having the right mindset than they did with their writing. She helped them with both and decided to start her own coaching and tutoring business.

Patricia works on the principle that we create our own reality and that we are responsible for everything that happens to us. She says that when we decide to be responsible, then life gets a whole lot easier! With great enthusiasm and gentle guidance, she helps people find their own creative path because she believes that if we all truly understand our power as spiritual beings, and we use that power ethically and effectively, then we really can create a world full of peace and harmony.

Herself a published author, she has never completely given up her training in language and literature. She not only writes books but helps others write their own stories through coaching and editing (www.MileHighEdit.com). She works with best-selling authors but also loves helping a first time author go through the process of writing a book. Patricia loves helping people express themselves better.

Now she helps students of all ages learn how to get the right mindset and keep it so that they can achieve any of their goals. She lives with her husband, daughter, and two dogs in Colorado where she helps change people's lives every day with Best Affirmations coaching and the *Best Affirmations Handbook* and the *Best Affirmations Workbook*.

BONUS!

We have just given you the best of the best tools available for making affirmations work for you. However, we also know how difficult it is to keep going. We all need accountability and someone to encourage us to keep us moving forward.

We have created a number of tools for you to make that happen. Go to www.bestaffirmations.com, and click on "Bonus." There you will find all sorts of goodies to help keep you on track. There are downloadable copies of Dr. Patricia Ross and Terri Levin, The Guru of Coaching® about the power of affirmations. This recording will get you jazzed about using affirmations everyday and all the time!

But the best tool we have for you is the *Best Affirmations Workbook: The 30-Day How-To Guide to Actively Create the Life you Want*. It has all the same helpful tools you just read about in the *Handbook*, but it puts them into a thirty-day program that holds you accountable. We can't give you the workbook entirely for free, but we are offering you an amazing discount. When you go to www.bestaffirmations.com, buy the workbook, and when you get to the checkout, enter this code: d7fcd9ef3f. It's a coupon for $10. The *Best Affirmations Workbook* retails for the incredibly low price of $14.95, but that means that you get the most powerful affirmation's tool imaginable for an unheard of $4.95!

Go to **www.bestaffirmations.com**. You can't afford *not* to take advantage of this offer.

Oh, and just because we know how powerful individual success coaching can be, call us today at (303) 938-1767 for a *free* thirty minute coaching session. Transform your life now!

We look forward to meeting you at BestAffirmations! Call us today!

BUY A SHARE OF THE FUTURE IN YOUR COMMUNITY

These certificates make great holiday, graduation and birthday gifts that can be personalized with the recipient's name. The cost of one S.H.A.R.E. or one square foot is $54.17. The personalized certificate is suitable for framing and will state the number of shares purchased and the amount of each share, as well as the recipient's name. The home that you participate in "building" will last for many years and will continue to grow in value.

THIS CERTIFIES THAT

YOUR NAME HERE

HAS INVESTED IN A HOME FOR A DESERVING FAMILY

1985-2005

TWENTY YEARS OF BUILDING FUTURES IN OUR
COMMUNITY ONE HOME AT A TIME

1200 SQUARE FOOT HOUSE @ $65,000 = $54.17 PER SQUARE FOOT
This certificate represents a tax-deductible donation. It has no cash value.

Here is a sample SHARE certificate:

YES, I WOULD LIKE TO HELP!

I support the work that Habitat for Humanity does and I want to be part of the excitement! As a donor, I will receive periodic updates on your construction activities but, more importantly, I know my gift will help a family in our community realize the dream of homeownership. **I would like to SHARE in your efforts against substandard housing in my community!** *(Please print below)*

PLEASE SEND ME _____ SHARES at $54.17 EACH = $ $_____

In Honor Of: _____

Occasion: (Circle One)   *HOLIDAY*   *BIRTHDAY*   *ANNIVERSARY*

         OTHER: _____

Address of Recipient: _____

Gift From: _____   *Donor Address:* _____

Donor Email: _____

I AM ENCLOSING A CHECK FOR $ $_____ PAYABLE TO HABITAT FOR HUMANITY <u>OR</u> PLEASE CHARGE MY VISA OR MASTERCARD *(CIRCLE ONE)*

Card Number _____ Expiration Date: _____

Name as it appears on Credit Card _____ Charge Amount $ _____

Signature _____

Billing Address _____

Telephone # Day _____   Eve _____

PLEASE NOTE: Your contribution is tax-deductible to the fullest extent allowed by law.
Habitat for Humanity • P.O. Box 1443 • Newport News, VA 23601 • 757-596-5553
www.HelpHabitatforHumanity.org